The Amazon Incubator

Grow Your Business or Hatch a New One

LESLEY HENSELL

PEAKPOINT
—— PRESS ——

Skyhorse Publishing books may be purchased in bulk at special discounts for sales promotion, corporate gifts, fund-raising, or educational purposes. Special editions can also be created to specifications. For details, contact the Special Sales Department, Skyhorse Publishing, 307 West 36th Street, 11th Floor, New York, NY 10018 or info@skyhorsepublishing.com.

Skyhorse® and Skyhorse Publishing® are registered trademarks of Skyhorse Publishing, Inc.®, a Delaware corporation.

Visit our website at www.skyhorsepublishing.com.

10 9 8 7 6 5 4 3 2 1

Library of Congress Cataloging-in-Publication Data is available on file.

Cover design by David Ter-Avanesyan

ISBN: 978-1-5107-7758-3
Ebook ISBN: 978-1-5107-7768-2

Printed in the United States of America

For Joe, Kelly, and Leah
The original Riverbenders

Contents

Part 4: Scale and Reach Your Goals 189

Introduction

Amazon is the most powerful business incubator in the history of the world.

Despite its audacity, this statement does not fully capture how Amazon empowers businesses. Amazon offers an incomparable opportunity for revenue and growth, whether a business is well-known or just getting off the ground. The e-commerce giant provides an unmatched sales channel for established brands. It enables solo entrepreneurs to launch products on a small scale and grow them into healthy enterprises. And it emboldens families to flip merchandise as a lucrative side-hustle.

You might expect to hear this feel-good perspective from gurus pushing online get-rich-quick strategies. But in this book, you are learning the advice and perspective of someone who spends their time on the "dark side" of Amazon, where businesses fail. Yet for every business that struggles, there are many more success stories that created healthy incomes and even long-term wealth.

Because Amazon offers such opportunity, cottage industries have sprung up to lure in new sellers and support those already on the platform. Gurus purport to teach sellers— whether newbies or established brands—how to turn Amazon's sales channel into a pot of gold. They promise riches at the cost of only five hours a week, or a long-term income for an initial investment of $1,000. Worst of all, they may label Amazon as an opportunity for passive income or mailbox money. I'm sad to say that these dreams, while tempting, are unrealistic.

> *Selling on Amazon is not easy. It is not passive income. And it is not for the faint of heart. Just because Amazon is an online marketplace doesn't mean that it's not a lot of work.*

I frequently rail against the difficulty of selling on Amazon. I speak out publicly about improvements Amazon should make to its seller ecosystem. Amazon's unique processes and policies make it hard for sellers to earn a consistent livelihood without making mistakes. Even innocent errors can lead to a seller's account being suspended or their bestselling item being taken down. The results can be extreme. I have known sellers who had heart attacks, threatened suicide, or sunk into depression when things went terribly wrong. I fight for clients who face both fair and unfair removal from the Amazon Marketplace. And yet, I am the first one to say that Amazon is the best sales channel for all sizes of brands and sellers to hawk their wares. It has no true rival.

My daily observances of Amazon sellers' painful misadventures have provided the impetus for this book. Because I spend so much time helping sellers who have stumbled on Amazon, I have developed a unique perspective on what it takes to be successful. I'm very clear about the opportunities for sellers, but my observations of what can go wrong encourage a healthy dose of goal setting, planning, strategy, and risk management.

My point of view is not only informed by watching other Amazon sellers. I've been a seller and built a business on Amazon too. And I love Amazon for the positive effects it has had on my family. These have been profound and life changing. In 2010, I was a self-employed consultant and, more importantly, a hands-on mom struggling to help a special-needs child and parent a toddler. My older son didn't fit in at school, and he was diagnosed with a slew of learning challenges and disabilities. My husband and I decided to homeschool him and enroll him in extensive (and expensive) therapies to address his underlying challenges. My past consulting work and the hands-on time with clients it required was no longer viable. But somehow, we had to pay for therapy.

Then, I heard about selling on Amazon. Back in 2010, the Amazon Marketplace was still the Wild West. Just about any product could be flipped after being sourced at a retail store, discount store, liquidator, or online outlet. Even better, the Fulfillment by Amazon (FBA) program was gearing up. This enables sellers to ship their inventory to Amazon fulfillment centers, rather than picking and packing orders to ship direct to buyers. When orders come in, Amazon ships them for the seller. It sounded like a dream come true.

I launched my Amazon business old-school, by selling books. I haunted every library book sale within fifty miles of my home, scooping up thousands of profitable books for just a few hundred dollars. Once I'd earned some cash from book sales, I reinvested those profits into retail arbitrage. I would drop by a discount store near me called Tuesday Morning and scan the barcode of every single product on the shelves. Each scan would pop up information like sales price, sales rank, and availability on Amazon. Usually, this would yield five to ten items that were highly profitable, and I would buy all available units. Then, I would methodically visit the fifteen-plus other Tuesday Morning stores in my metro area. I would quickly run in and out of each location to buy only those items I had already identified as money-makers. In a couple of days of sourcing, I would bring home several SUV-loads of products to resell.

This same model worked for all kinds of discount stores and liquidators near me. I flipped everything from ready-to-eat spinach dahl and turkey brining bags to high-end blenders, creepy-eyeball Halloween candy, and children's bedding. If it made a profit, I would buy it and flip it on the Amazon Marketplace.

The book sale and retail arbitrage sourcing models worked great for my family. I took care of the boys while my husband was at his full-time job. I could shop for inventory at night or on weekends while my husband was home with the kids. Then, we would set aside weekend time to prep and pack the inventory for shipment to the Amazon FBA warehouse. The kids helped and learned valuable skills. (Yes, a two-year-old can put barcode stickers on inventory, with the right supervision!) My boys still put in hours at my Amazon business today.

Amazon didn't make our family rich during this busy time in our lives. But we earned enough money to pay for therapy, and then to fund tuition at a special needs school. We hit our financial goals and then some, all while giving our children the quality time they needed. It was a beautiful solution, and I will always be grateful for the opportunity Amazon gave me when I faced difficult circumstances.

After three years of homeschooling, my older kiddo was ready to go back to school. And I was ready for a new challenge.

I continued to operate my Amazon business, and I launched an Amazon consulting business using the same skills that I had once leveraged for traditional consulting. I combined this experience with the knowledge I amassed over three years of aggressively selling online.

Today, with the help of my business partner, Joe Zalta, I've grown that consulting knowledge into an eighty-five-person company that helps Amazon sellers with a wide range of problems. There's a reason I say that my business works on the dark side. Other Amazon service firms focus on the fun parts of selling, like launching products or developing ad campaigns. In contrast, we help sellers with some of the most profound and difficult challenges that can be faced by an Amazon business. I have heard clients weep during our phone calls. They have raged, cursed, and sat in shocked silence. These reactions are valid for sellers faced with laying off team members and going bankrupt.

Why were their responses to their Amazon problems so extreme? For many of my clients, Amazon provides the majority of their revenue and profits. Without it, they are lost. Selling on Amazon can be disheartening and frustrating. The platform has its own set of rules, regulations, and operating procedures. My clients face everything from suspension of their selling accounts to permanent holds on their funds to loss of their products by Amazon fulfillment centers. The list of potential pitfalls is endless.

Despite the constant litany of challenges brought to me by sellers each day, almost all these individuals still desire to sell on Amazon. They, too, understand the powerful engine that the world's second-largest retailer puts behind their products. And just as I've listened with tears in my eyes as sellers mourn their lost Amazon businesses, I've celebrated with others who hit massive revenue goals or sold their companies for millions.

In the following pages, you will learn more about how to be a big success on the Amazon platform—the right way. You will get the information you need to:

- choose how you sell on Amazon
- create your Amazon goals
- build an Amazon business plan
- outsource
- develop standard operating procedures
- and more

By starting with the end in mind, you can ensure that your Amazon business will be designed to win. You can avoid the failures and disappointments that too many Amazon sellers have fought through.

Dream big. Then use this book to develop your own strategic plan. Leverage Amazon to hatch your business and grow your dream into the best version of itself.

Part 1

What's So Great about Amazon?

CHAPTER 1

Amazon, the E-Commerce Powerhouse

If you can only sell in one place, sell on Amazon. It gives you access to more than 300 million buyers, one of the world's most impressive fulfillment networks, and a host of tools that can drive your success.

That's why almost 2 million companies have seller accounts on Amazon. They leverage the world's largest marketplace to grow their businesses and drive revenue. But with so many competitors and such a wide selection of products already available, does it still make sense to sell on Amazon right now? Each year, the difficulties of the Amazon Marketplace loom larger. Sellers must have thicker skin and deeper pockets. You can hear it in countless discussions across all segments of the business world:

- Small entrepreneurs feel like they must work harder than ever to source and sell products that will yield a profit. Plus, they face the reality that Amazon expects its sellers to operate like traditional businesses, not fly-by-night side-hustles. This means accounting, recordkeeping and other expensive, boring tasks are required. These small sellers wonder if it would just be easier to sell on eBay.

- Resellers worry that an increase in competitors on Amazon will force them to mark down prices or leave them with unsold goods languishing in their warehouses. They consider shifting some of their efforts to Walmart or other online marketplaces, or perhaps leaving Amazon altogether.
- US sellers see a hoard of overseas companies listing low-cost goods on Amazon. This increases fears that domestic sellers will lose both the short-term battle and the long-term war against foreign competitors.
- Brands wonder if it's worth the struggle to control the Amazon channel, since they have limited power over how resellers source, offer, and price their products. They are tempted to stop selling on Amazon and focus on their own proprietary websites and other channels.

Yet for all but a few truly frustrated sellers, the threats to abandon the Amazon Marketplace ring hollow. It is unsurprising that the largest online retail marketplace with the most attractive features for buyers would carry the most challenges for sellers. The opportunity is just too great for businesses to abandon or ignore.

What Makes One Sales Channel Superior to the Rest?

There are limitless channels where sellers and brands can market their products. Today's sellers usually spread their product offerings across some mix of online marketplaces, their own websites, social media platforms, mobile apps, brick-and-mortar stores, and wholesalers. For most businesses, just one or two of these channels creates much of their revenue.

With so many options available, it's important for companies to carefully evaluate where to spend their time and energy. Resources are finite, whether you're a newly launched entrepreneurial venture or a long-established brand. If you can afford to launch and manage only one sales channel, it should probably be Amazon.

Since its founding in 1994, the company has built a retail juggernaut. In early 2023, Amazon was the world's fifth-largest company in terms of market capitalization, while ranking second globally in revenue. Amazon's total revenue is still behind that of rival Walmart, thanks to the latter's massive network of physical stores in addition to its online presence. Nevertheless, Amazon has been gaining steadily.

Gradually, the company developed competencies that eventually became advantages over the competition. These strengths are many and varied, and the chances of them being quickly overtaken by a newcomer are small to none. This is where Amazon is so different from other sales channels available to sellers and brands. With Amazon, a seller can take advantage of the infrastructure, marketing, and cachet of a trillion-dollar company. The seller's goods are displayed on Amazon.com the same way Amazon's own products—and those of massive international brands—are displayed. Even the smallest of sellers can leverage Amazon's full-featured advertising and promotions program, distribution and fulfillment network, and built-in audience. Nowhere else on Earth—and at no other time in history—has this been possible.

What You Need—and What You Don't

Imagine launching a consumer products company today, with the goal of selling and fulfilling orders via your own branded website. You perform market research, obtain financing, and manufacture goods. Now what? To have any hope of success, you would need:

- Warehouse space to store inventory
- A website with e-commerce capabilities
- Advertising and marketing campaigns to drive traffic to that website
- A customer experience team to answer customer queries and complaints
- A third-party logistics provider or in-house team to pick, pack and ship customer orders, as well as handle returns and refunds
- And a whole lot more

On the surface, selling via your own website sounds attractive. It offers your brand complete control over the entire customer experience from end to end. But how does your brand drive traffic to its website? Is a multimillion-dollar marketing and advertising budget available? Is fulfillment reliable? Can the company afford to offer the fast and free shipping that consumers expect today?

Depending on how sellers set up their businesses, Amazon can eliminate the needed investment for most of this expensive infrastructure. Instead, sellers can take advantage of some of the world's largest and most impressive capabilities around advertising, marketing, warehousing, order fulfillment, and more.

A Built-In Customer Base of More than 300 Million

A company's branded Shopify website starts with zero customers and zero website traffic.

Amazon racks up around 2 billion site visits per month. Of course, these visitors don't all see one specific product; they look at millions of products. Nevertheless, the site has built-in traffic and buyers that an individual Shopify store would take decades to obtain.

There are more than 200 million Amazon Prime subscribers around the globe, and another 100 million account holders who do not have Prime membership. Approximately 150 million Prime subscribers live in the United States, meaning there is lots of room to grow in Amazon's international marketplaces. No other retailer, platform, or marketplace can boast these tremendous numbers, nor Amazon's level of customer loyalty. Keep in mind that 200 million is the number of Prime subscriptions, many of which are shared between multiple household members who buy on Amazon. (There are four people on mine!)

Amazon's Prime program is arguably its most powerful driver of business on the Marketplace. Prime launched back in 2005. It requires an annual subscription fee, which in 2023 was $139 per year, or $14.99 per month. Over time, the company has added a host of high-value benefits in return for the annual paid subscription. Most Prime members report that their favorite of these benefits is Prime shipping, a promise of free two-day delivery for hundreds of thousands of products. In many metropolitan areas, Prime members also can expect free one-day or even same-day delivery for a wide range of goods. This has made Amazon exceptionally sticky for consumers who have grown dependent on the company, its website, its wide product selection, and its user-friendly app. With just a few clicks, customers can compare prices and place an order from anywhere. Why navigate the crowds and fight for parking at a retailer miles away, if Amazon can simply deliver what you need? Many consumers conduct price checks on the Amazon mobile app while standing in the aisles of competing brick-and-mortar stores. If Amazon's offer is cheaper, the consumer will buy right from the app, save money, and skip the checkout line. For sellers, this means their products are not just competing with other online offerings. They directly compete with brick-and-mortar retailers as well.

Amazon once billed itself as "The Everything Store," and that reputation has remained. Because Prime members know they can find everything from clothing and beauty items to auto parts and housewares, Amazon is often their first choice for shopping. Prime members also know they have access to exclusive deals and discounts not available to nonmembers.

When Amazon built these features and established this massive customer base, it created unmatched value for sellers. Here is a shocker: 81 percent of US Internet users aged eighteen to thirty-four have a Prime membership. According to Amazon software provider Jungle Scout, 61 percent of US consumers start their online product searches on Amazon. And according to online shopping aggregator Ibotta, more than half of consumers shop more on mobile than in-store. Put these statistics together, and it's easy to see the massive value of the Amazon Prime customer base. The average US Prime subscriber spends about $1,400 on Amazon per year. And because they pay for Prime membership and become virtually addicted to the ease of shopping on Amazon, these buyers purchase more each year on the Marketplace than they would without their Prime membership. This adds up to more opportunities for Amazon sellers.

And let's not forget Prime Day sales. During these summer events, Amazon rolls out thousands of special deals for Prime members. In 2023, Prime Day gross sales topped $12.9 billion on the purchase of more than 375 million items. Much of that revenue went to Amazon third-party sellers, who used the opportunity to offer discounts that helped turn over their inventory, while exposing their brands to new consumers.

Fair Competition on an Unbiased Platform

Almost anybody can sell almost any product on Amazon. Contrast this with the fierce challenges of trying to launch a novel product in a brick-and-mortar store. Imagine a new brand that wants to introduce its low-carb breakfast cereal to a grocery store chain. First, the brand must decide which chain of stores to pitch its products. This decision should be based on extensive market research and a full competitive analysis across multiple retailers. Then, the brand must search for the breakfast cereal buyer somewhere on the breakfast foods desk at the retailer's massive headquarters office. (Or should they approach the low-carb/keto products buyer? It's a mystery!) Next, the brand must convince the breakfast cereal buyer why this new product should get valuable, limited shelf space in place of powerful national brands that have a large, established consumer base and a proven track record of sales.

If you think this sounds extremely difficult, you are correct! Placing products into national retail chains that have significant foot traffic is not just daunting. It requires specific expertise, an up-to-date contact list, superhuman persistence, and thick skin.

Contrast the above brick-and-mortar retail scenario with the process for "placing" a product on Amazon.com. The steps are much easier:

1. Set up a seller account on Amazon by filling out basic information on the Seller Central website.
2. Complete account verification, which requires the seller to provide identity documents and financial documentation.
3. List products on Amazon. This may require an extra step or two for permission to sell goods in certain categories that may present extra risk to consumers (e.g., baby, toys, luxury beauty), but that hurdle generally can be overcome.

Simply listing products on Amazon does not guarantee they will sell. Much more hard work is required. But Amazon generally won't block companies from using its platform, nor will it always declare that certain categories of products are "full up" and no additional competitors are welcome.

There are exclusions. Amazon will not allow the listing of specific goods it deems as "Restricted," such as CBD products, vaping pens, Confederate flag merchandise, and supplements with iffy ingredients. But these are the exceptions and most definitely not the rule. In addition, Amazon blocks bad-actor companies regularly. When a "bad guy" tries to register to sell on Amazon, the company has effective verification systems to block their initial enrollment. If the fraudulent seller makes it past the initial hurdles, Amazon will usually catch them after they list prohibited products, fail to ship items, or otherwise mistreat customers or other sellers. (More on this in Chapter 9.)

Other than that, sellers on Amazon are welcome to compete with anybody. There are no sacred cows—not even Amazon itself. Want to sell fancy coffee beans that go head-to-head with a hundred-year-old brand? Do it! Does your specially formulated mascara outlast the beauty brands found in every grocery and drugstore? Launch it! Did you build a product that can take on the Amazon Echo? List it!

Most products on Amazon are offered by multiple sellers. The competition can be fierce, with a wide range of resellers duking it out to get the next sale. For the most part, this competition is encouraged. This is not the most attractive selling model out there, but it is available to those who don't mind going toe-to-toe with other Amazon sellers.

An Unmatched Distribution and Fulfillment Network

Storing, picking, packing, and shipping orders can be costly. That's why many sellers prefer to outsource this function to Amazon.

As of early 2023, consulting firm MWPVL International estimated that Amazon operated 1,285 distribution facilities in the United States, with another 231 in the planning stages. When built out, this will encompass nearly 500 million square feet across US fulfillment centers, returns processing centers, Prime Now hubs, inbound receiving centers, sortation centers, delivery stations, airport hubs, and manufacturing facilities. Across the rest of the globe are another thousand-plus facilities totaling more than 200 million additional square feet either actively in use or in the planning and construction phases.

In 2021, investment firm UBS estimated that Amazon had fulfillment centers within one hour of 77 percent of Americans. The company has continued to invest in additional facilities, including its Prime Air in-house cargo airlines. In early 2023, more than two hundred flights per day helped the company speed along deliveries throughout the United States. Add in more than forty thousand semi-trucks, hundreds of thousands of last-mile vans and middle-mile trucks, and you have a logistics network rivalled only by retail carriers with long histories such as FedEx, UPS, and the US Postal Service. (And keep in mind that Amazon still uses all three of these carriers to assist with deliveries as well.)

What does all this mean for Amazon sellers? Buyers can receive products—fast. Also, Amazon can access, either via its own logistics organization or through deals with partner carriers, cheaper shipping rates than most sellers and brands. The savings are passed along to sellers who rely on Amazon to ship their products. For example, I know one large-volume seller whose best corporate shipping rate with FedEx was 10 percent more than their shipping costs with Amazon. Plus, by relying on Amazon FBA for most of their shipping needs, the business could keep its warehouse and fulfillment employee head counts lower.

Massive Marketing Infrastructure

Trillion-dollar companies are marketing powerhouses. Amazon is no exception. The company runs Super Bowl ads, hires celebrity spokespeople, and features ubiquitous branding. In 2022, Amazon spent more than $42 billion on marketing. This included online advertising, TV ads, social media, and more. Amazon spent $20 billion on ads in 2022, making it the biggest advertiser in history.

When billions in ads and marketing initiatives drive buyers to Amazon.com, sellers and brands on the Marketplace benefit. No other platform comes close to that level of advertising support.

Even Amazon's affiliate marketing program leads the world among affiliate marketing options. Amazon Associates has more than nine hundred thousand members driving traffic to Amazon.com and encouraging the purchase of products.

Worldwide Reach for Sellers of All Sizes

Selling internationally can be daunting. For companies that intend to sell at high volumes overseas, significant infrastructure will be needed over time.

But for Amazon sellers, there is an easier way to test the viability of their products in foreign markets. The Amazon Global Selling program enables companies to sell their products across twenty-three countries: Austria, Australia, Belgium, Brazil, Canada, China, France, Germany, India, Ireland, Italy, Japan, Luxembourg, Mexico, Poland, Saudi Arabia, Singapore, Spain, Sweden, Turkey, the Netherlands, the United Kingdom, and the United States.

Selling overseas with Amazon still requires commitment and hard work, from setting up Marketplace accounts in foreign countries to registering for the European Union Value Added Tax (VAT) and establishing a fulfillment strategy. Amazon's FBA warehouses around the world, however, certainly simplify at least one major aspect of the selling equation. Amazon account managers in growing market-places also regularly provide support to sellers who wish to expand overseas.

Market Testing in the Real World—at Scale

Angry Orange Odor Eliminator was a novel idea for a cleaning product. This strongly scented spray could neutralize yucky pet odors and remove stains. It really, really worked. But the product was the brainchild of an entrepreneur without a well-known brand or retail presence. He was a small fish in the very large pond of household cleaning products.

Instead of fighting to get the item into brick-and-mortar stores, the entrepreneur decided to launch it on Amazon. Buyers found the product and gave it excellent reviews. Repeat buyers came back for more. Revenue grew. The brand expanded and morphed into a top cleaning product on Amazon. After several years, it became a classic started-on-Amazon success story, and the brand sold for $1.4 million. (It has since scaled to more than $20 million in annual sales.) Why did the seller succeed? He had access to a massive consumer marketplace, where he could test changes to his product, advertising, and marketing efforts and see the effects in real-time.

With its built-in customer base, Amazon is an unparalleled venue to test new products at scale. Millions of potential buyers can be leveraged to test ads, listing images, product variations, and more.

In addition, the existing Amazon catalog offers endless market research opportunities. Using software designed specifically for Amazon sellers, you can analyze the sales history for opposing products. These tools even rate the quality of Amazon listing detail pages, revealing possible inroads for enterprising competitors.

Launching Specialty Products That Would Fail in the "Real World"

Specialty goods are, by definition, hard to find. These include everything from hobby supplies and replacement parts to products that address specific medical conditions and more.

Specialty products are a great option for selling on Amazon. While you may not find enough customers locally to buy your unique bee pollen–infused energy drink, there may be enough buyers across the entire United States to make your products profitable.

Consider the seller of baseball training aids designed for teenagers playing at the select level. His target market is extremely specific. Across the United States, thousands of baseball players may be interested in this product. But in a local area, it would be difficult to find enough players to support the item. Even brick-and-mortar sporting goods chains may not bring in enough qualified leads. But on Amazon? With the right keywords and advertising strategy, more than enough traffic is served up to make this seller's baseball training aids a profitable hit. Even the most special of specialty products has a chance to thrive.

You can create this same kind of unique success on Amazon. But first, it's time to define what you consider a success in your own life—and your own Amazon business.

Chapter 1 Summary

- If you can only sell on one marketplace or sales channel, choose Amazon.
- For sellers, Amazon's most powerful draw is its 200 million Prime members. This loyal audience tends to shop on Amazon first for new purchases, and these customers spend more on Amazon than they would without a Prime membership.
- Even the smallest seller can draw in buyers and provide a best-in-class customer experience, since they benefit from Amazon's position as the world's largest advertiser and fulfillment house.

What about you?

1. Think about the types of products you have available to sell, or those you wish to sell. Are they a good fit for Amazon? Why or why not?
2. What do you consider your top sales channels, now or in the future? Sales channels might include various marketplaces such as Amazon, eBay, Mercari, and more, as well as retail stores, wholesale, and liquidation. What are the strengths and weaknesses of each?
3. How could you use the Amazon marketplace as a vehicle for market testing your products? Might you try selling two similar items with different colors or features to see which performs best?

4. Are there specialty product ideas you've had in the past that were not viable because of a lack of demand? Would they be viable on a large marketplace like Amazon? Can you determine whether there is enough demand by launching a test run?

CHAPTER 2

What Does Success Look Like for Your Amazon Business?

Selling on Amazon is a get-rich-quick scheme. Selling on Amazon is the path to a four-hour workweek featuring a laptop, a fruity drink with an umbrella, and a beach. Selling on Amazon is a necessity for established brands, even though they are destined for pain.

There are varying degrees of truth to each of these statements. There is no single way to sell on Amazon. The company's third-party Marketplace offers opportunities for sellers to create their own style of business. This enterprise can be leveraged to accomplish a wide range of goals, whether you are an individual selling goods out of your home or a multi-million-dollar corporation looking to dominate every possible channel for your winning products.

No matter the goal, however, one thing is for sure: Amazon is not a set-it-and-forget-it, get-rich-quick scheme. It is not passive income. And it is not mailbox money.

Before talking about what Amazon can be for you and your business, let's explore what Amazon most definitely is not.

Who Wants a Lamborghini?

Long before the 2020 COVID-19 pandemic sent businesses to a work-from-home model, Amazon gurus touted the Marketplace as the ultimate opportunity for freedom. Through books, online courses, YouTube videos, and "coaching," the gurus preached that:

- Anyone could invest just $1,000 and quickly make millions on Amazon.
- Amazon is the ultimate work-from-anywhere solution, which allows you to live in exotic locations while collecting your passive Amazon income.
- See my hot cars, shiny mansion, and rocking body? Amazon did that—and I hardly had to work for it.

Unfortunately, thousands upon thousands of would-be sellers have bought into these hollow dreams—for a price. They may have paid for classes and coaching. They may have sunk their life savings into inventory that never sold. Or they may have paid someone to "do it all" for them, which resulted in huge money losses, or worse.

These schemes, scams, and broken dreams have given the Amazon Marketplace a bad reputation in some circles. Entrepreneurs and hard-working hustlers either buy into the fantasy, or they see it as a potential nightmare. Are all coaching programs and software offerings a scam? No. But there are enough bad actors out there to create a great deal of risk for wannabe Amazon entrepreneurs.

Meanwhile, the corporate world has its own fears and frustrations with the Amazon channel. Some bypass selling on Amazon, believing they are protecting their brand and their pricing structure. Others avoid controlling their product listings and brand image on Amazon, thinking they are somehow depriving the Marketplace and resellers of credibility needed to resell their products.

All of these concerns and consternations are valid. The problems are real. The challenges are frustrating, whether you're a small business or an enormous one. But that doesn't mean Amazon should not be part of your strategic plan to reach your ultimate goals.

What's Better than Hot Cars and a Four-Hour Workweek?

The dream of earning millions for little effort sounds attractive. But as with any other business initiative, it's not a realistic, long-term strategy.

Done right, the Amazon Marketplace offers third-party sellers something more attractive: a sustainable business with the potential to build your brand, create strong margins, and expand over time. How you set up such a business should be determined by your personal goals and chosen lifestyle. Consider the following Amazon seller avatars and which is most attractive to you, over the short term and the long haul. By choosing an avatar—or mixing and matching two that work for you—you can better envision your Amazon journey and what it has in store for you.

Common Amazon Seller Avatars
The Side Hustler.

Amazon provides an ideal opportunity for folks who like to supplement their income with a side hustle. Many full-time sellers on the platform—including some who move millions of dollars in products a year—started out as side hustlers.

Side hustlers include folks who flip products on Amazon via retail arbitrage (RA) and online arbitrage (OA). That means they purchase products, either from brick-and-mortar retailers or online stores, and then resell them on the Amazon Marketplace. RA and OA sellers might flip the hottest Christmas toy that they find at every Walmart in a hundred-mile radius. Or they might make money from a few "replens," or replenishable products. As an example, I knew a seller who resold canned molasses they found at Walmart stores in the South. Apparently, the product was carried regionally, making it hard to find in other parts of the country. Some replens sellers make a nice side income (think $1,000 to $2,000 per month, net) by reselling just five to ten replenishable products on Amazon that don't have much competition from other sellers. Some side hustlers might also sell a product they created on Amazon, or they may resell stock purchased from wholesalers or local businesses without an online presence.

For side hustlers, the point is the income. They are product agnostic. They don't care about specializing in a certain category of product. They aren't on a mission to change the world with the products they sell. They simply want a healthy side income that they can make relatively easily and in their extra time.

The Brand Builder.

Thousands of small brands have been launched on Amazon.com by Marketplace sellers. These businesses are typically sole proprietorships or family enterprises that create a unique private-label product. Many Brand Builders have an interest or expertise in a specific category, or they are focused on solving a specific problem. For example, I've met Brand Builders who specialize in products for children with autism, babies with feeding issues, crafters who use unique materials, adults with rare medical conditions, and more. Some Brand Builders resell products in their niche, alongside their own private-label offerings. They may be on a mission to make the world a better place. Or they may simply want financial freedom for their family, while also doing work they feel is important and needed. Brand Builders may create their brands as a side-hustle at the outset, and then later quit their 9-to-5 job so they can focus on their brands as they become financially viable and create real income.

The Lifestyle Impresario.

These are folks who long for a nomadic lifestyle, a ton of free time, or hot cars and over-the-top vacations. Lifestyle Impresarios typically develop private-label products they sell on Amazon. They invest aggressively into advertising and promotions, with the hope of creating cash flow as soon as possible after product launch. Their ultimate goal? Developing multiple streams of income on Amazon. They usually aren't excited about a product's features and benefits. Rather, they are focused on which product can offer them the highest sales volume and profit margins. In addition, Lifestyle Impresarios are big believers in outsourcing. They either find highly skilled virtual assistants (VAs) to run a portion of their business's day-to-day operations, outsource to trustworthy agencies, or hire and train to fill these positions.

The Classic Entrepreneur.

These sellers are open to an "all-of-the-above" business model. They are dealmakers who understand that profits are made when the product is bought, not when it is sold. They might find low-cost liquidation deals hiding at a manufacturing facility that recently changed their product packaging. Or they might strike a licensing deal with a major brand and arrange for the manufacturing of new products featuring profitable cartoon characters. They aren't too concerned about selling in a certain category or solving a specific problem for a target market. Rather, they solve business problems and seek to provide the products that the marketplace demands.

The Corporate Defensive Line.

Brands that were not built on Amazon often see the e-commerce giant as an enemy. They dislike the Marketplace for countless reasons. They cannot control the pricing of their products, whether sold directly by Amazon's retail operation or by third-party sellers. They have difficulty preventing random sellers from offering their products, which may be perceived as harmful to the brand. In other words, they struggle to control their products' distribution and their brand's image. If they don't want to sell on the Amazon platform themselves, these companies play defense. They take whatever measures they can to ensure their brands are properly represented, their product pages are accurate and attractive, and that bad actors are not offering their products.

The Corporate Growth Hacker.

Many established brands have a manager or director specifically assigned to oversee the Amazon channel. Those who understand Amazon can work in an entrepreneurial manner—even inside a large corporate conglomerate—to make the most of the Marketplace. They research and strategize to ensure their product mix on Amazon maximizes their sales. They carefully manage inventory to make sure they never run out of popular items. They utilize the same growth-oriented tools as private-label sellers, such as Amazon advertising and special Prime deals. And in some cases, they create Amazon-specific packaging or product bundles to drive Amazon sales while not competing with the goods they ship to retail stores or sell on other online marketplaces. The Corporate Growth Hacker knows that, managed carefully, their Amazon channel can become one of the most important in the company.

The Big Brand Product Launcher.

For established brands, launching new products can be risky and expensive, even online. The best product managers know that they can use the Amazon Marketplace to test their product name, description, photos, advertising strategy, and more. I've met people who work inside some of the country's largest consumer goods companies. They consider Amazon an incubator for their hottest new ideas. They test pricing, coupons, and deals as well, to see what might move buyers to choose their newest product over an older model or the competition. Once they have used Amazon to tweak their new offerings, they roll these products out to other sales channels more successfully than they would have without a substantial proving ground.

What Avatar Feels Right to You?

What is your attraction to selling on Amazon? What are your goals?

The entire point of launching a new entrepreneurial venture is to meet specific goals. Starting up and running any new business—whether a solo gig, a small family enterprise, or a business unit inside of a larger corporation—requires capital, hard work, lost sleep, risk tolerance, and a strong constitution. It's not worth the time and effort unless this investment is made in service of a larger purpose.

To choose the right business model for yourself, you must be realistic about what you'd like your life to look like:

- How many hours are you willing to work right now? What about in one year, three years or five years? Can you tolerate an eighty-hour work week, like the Classic Entrepreneur? Can you work nights and weekends while trying to turn your side gig into a full-time business, like the Side Hustler?
- How comfortable are you hiring and managing a team, whether that's a group of full-time employees, outside agencies or virtual assistants? Brand Builders

and Lifestyle Impresarios can't reach their goals without these management skills.

- Which day-to-day activities of an Amazon business sound exciting to you? Are you a creative force, a nose-to-the-grindstone researcher, or an inventory expert? Which parts of the job that you love will add the most value over time?

- Think about your personal life and current work life. Where would you like to spend your time now and in the future?

- Is there a charitable, political, educational, religious, or other cause that you are passionate about? What about a hobby or sport? Should any of these inform the products you sell? Will you donate a portion of your time or profits?

- What kind of income is needed to fund the lifestyle you want? Consider what it would take to pay off any current debt and pay your monthly bills. What kind of cash would your business need to generate over time to give you ultimate freedom to make life changes that you want over time? These questions are particularly key for Lifestyle Impresarios and Brand Builders.

Chapter 2 Summary

- Before you can find the right Amazon avatar for yourself, you need to understand your financial and lifestyle goals.

- There are a wide range of avatars, which can be mixed and matched. Choosing an avatar or two can help a new seller envision their future Amazon business.

What about you?

1. Calculate your personal debt and monthly expenses. What would it take in the short- and long-term to create true financial freedom? Can an Amazon business provide that?

2. Think about the lifestyle you'd like over one year, three years, five years, and long-term. Do you want to retire? When? What does your family situation look like? How will you spend your time?

3. Commit your thoughts to paper. Jotting down a profile of what you'd like your life to look like will give you clearer ideas as you hatch your Amazon business.

CHAPTER 3

Unlock the Right Opportunity for You

There is no "right" way to sell on Amazon. That much we learned in Chapter 2.

This may be news to those who make their living off the Amazon seller ecosystem. Hyper-competitive hustlers, e-commerce gurus, account management agencies, brand incubators, and Goliath sellers—each has developed their formula for Amazon dominance. And in their eyes, that formula is the only path to success. In reality, there is no end to the ways to run a lucrative Amazon business. The trick is to build something that works for you and can be sustained over time. For new Amazon entrepreneurs and brands alike, it all starts with one basic decision. Should you be an Amazon vendor or a third-party seller?

In this chapter, I will try to persuade you that third-party selling is the only way you should go, with minimal exceptions. Once you've made up your own mind, you can further refine your ideal Amazon avatar and build a customized model for your business.

There are two primary buckets that hold the products sold on Amazon:

- Vendor, which is also known as first-party or retail sales. Vendors manage their Amazon relationship in the Amazon Vendor Central app.
- Third-party seller, which is managed in the Amazon Seller Central app.

The 3P vs. 1P Smackdown

On Amazon, "1P" refers to members of the Amazon Vendor program. These companies act as wholesale suppliers to Amazon, the same way they might sell products to a brick-and-mortar retailer. Amazon Vendors might be brands selling directly to Amazon, or they can be distributors of multiple brands and product lines.

Amazon chooses which items to offer from a vendor's catalog of goods and submits purchase orders to the vendor. The items listed for sale show that they are "sold by" and "shipped by" Amazon.com, making Amazon the seller of record. Amazon also decides the pricing for these goods. In total, vendor products make up about one-third of retail sales on Amazon. Not everyone can be a vendor on Amazon. The program is by invitation only, but with the right connections a new brand can wrangle an invite.

In contrast, "3P" refers to third-party sellers on the Amazon Marketplace. These businesses are responsible for about two-thirds of retail sales on Amazon. They are the sellers of record for their items. Sellers operate independently of Amazon, choosing which products to sell on the Marketplace and at what prices. Any brand that sells legal products can set up an Amazon seller account. The process does not require an invitation.

The Pros and Cons of Being a 3P Amazon Seller

Amazon third-party sellers can choose between two fulfillment methods for their sales:

Fulfillment by Amazon (FBA). 3P sellers ship their inventory to Amazon fulfillment centers, where orders are stored, picked, packed, and shipped by Amazon for a fee. This carries the added benefit of the Amazon Prime badge, since FBA items almost always qualify for free shipping to Prime members. While Amazon refuses to release statistics about the Prime badge, research companies and active sellers will attest that having the Prime badge dramatically increases sales.

Fulfillment by Merchant (FBM). 3P sellers either ship orders themselves or use a third-party logistics firm to store and fulfill orders from Amazon customers. With FBM, Amazon earns its cut as a "referral fee" on each purchase. Think of it as a sales commission. The referral fee also applies to FBA orders.

Amazon third-party sellers have more power and control over their brand on the platform:

- They choose which products to offer and at what price.
- They can launch products on Amazon without approval.

- They can change pricing whenever they wish.
- They can offer products by FBA, FBM, or both.
- They control their own advertising campaigns, coupons, and other brand-building strategies.
- If they sell their own brand on Amazon, they may control their listing detail pages and enhanced brand content, which can be beautifully built out to prompt more sales.

With power and control, however, comes additional responsibility. For example, third-party sellers are expected to answer buyer messages. If orders are FBM, sellers must provide customer service including returns and refunds.

In addition, 3P sellers must keep a close eye on their FBA inventory. Items in the Amazon Fulfillment Centers are regularly damaged or lost. Sellers have to file claims to be reimbursed for this inventory, or they must hire a service provider to do it for them. There are also significant fees associated with selling via FBA. Sellers must stay on top of these fees and understand how they affect bottom-line profitability.

Finally, 3P sellers are subject to a much higher level of enforcement by Amazon's risk management departments. Products or even seller accounts can be suspended based on buyer complaints or violations of the rules. Vendors and their products can be suspended as well, but this happens much less frequently.

The Pros and Cons of the 1P Vendor Program

Selling 1P is the easiest and most hands-off method of selling on Amazon. That's what makes it attractive to some vendors, especially those who run very high volumes of products through Amazon. They ship pallets of goods to an Amazon fulfillment center, or Amazon even picks up the goods from the vendor's warehouse. And then the vendor is hands-off for orders, fulfillment, returns, customer service, and the like.

In some cases, vendors act as drop-shippers for Amazon and fulfill orders themselves out of their own warehouses. From the buyer's perspective, the order appears to ship from Amazon, even though it does not.

In either case, the vendor does not decide the offer price for their goods. Amazon does—and Amazon doesn't honor minimum advertised pricing (MAP) programs. MAP is part of doing business for many brands, which contractually require retailers to sell their items at a set price or above. Other websites or retailers can become angry when Amazon is undercutting them on price, which can lead to tricky negotiations for future purchase orders.

Amazon also may choose to stop offering products that are important to the vendor. Perhaps Amazon was not making a profit on a particular item, or their automated systems decided a new addition to the catalog didn't make sense. This can be painful to a vendor, which may have been counting on revenue from new product launches or past bestsellers that Amazon no longer wants to offer.

Amazon truly has all the power over vendors. It also plays hardball when negotiating purchase prices, and it automatically rejects many requests for price increases from vendors, even when those price increases are the result of inflation. In addition, as part of its vendor agreement, Amazon pushes for hefty fees and allowances. These include a marketing co-op, returns allowance, overstock allowance, damage allowance, and freight allowance. These fees can really add up, making the bottom line less healthy than expected.

Where does the vendor program make sense? Brands with large, heavy items usually end up better off financially as Amazon vendors. The fees for bulky products on the 3P seller side are substantial and can make selling these products unprofitable. In addition, vendors benefit from higher sales velocity that comes with the Amazon Prime badge, as well as Amazon's more favorable algorithmic treatment of "sold by Amazon" products in search results.

As far as Amazon seller avatars go, the 1P program is most likely to be embraced by the Corporate Defensive Line. Other avatars are more likely to go the 3P route.

Vendor Horror Stories

Selling on both the 3P and 1P sides comes with challenges. But some of the difficulties that are exclusive to the vendor side can be a huge turn-off. Consider these scenarios:

- A snack food vendor shipped a product to an Amazon Fulfillment Center (FC). Amazon then put about $40,000 worth of the product on a truck to send to another warehouse. The truck was involved in an accident, and the product was destroyed. The delivery service (hired by Amazon) filed a claim with its insurance company, and the vendor was told to expect a resolution and reimbursement in three to five business days. Six months later, no money had come. It took hiring my consulting firm, which performed a great deal of work, to get reimbursed for the products Amazon had ordered and accepted.

- A longtime Amazon vendor of beauty products had many shipments that were not received in a timely manner at the Amazon fulfillment centers. The vendor filed claim after claim, and Amazon eventually received the inventory and paid the vendor for the items. These payments, however, were made after two or three months. This didn't stop Amazon from automatically deducting a quick-pay discount of 2 percent. This discount should not have been taken unless the invoice was paid in less than thirty days. The unfair discounts added up to more than $300,000. The vendor hired my company and asked us to go after the most recent two years of improper discounts. After multiple communications with Amazon executives, we helped the vendor shake $126,000 out of Amazon. Amazon refused to refund the beauty firm for the balance, saying it should have pursued the matter sooner.

- An electronics vendor sold Amazon a million dollars' worth of high-end smartphones. On Black Friday, Walmart put the same model of smartphone on sale for cost, and Amazon decided to match the price. Even after the Black Friday sale ended at Walmart, Amazon continued to sell the phone for the at-cost price. When Amazon took a bath on the item, it came to the vendor and demanded "straight pay" of $100,000 to make up for the loss in profitability, even though the vendor had no control over the price Amazon charged for the phone.

- A pet accessory manufacturer sold its unique and colorful dog feeders to Amazon. For an unknown reason, Amazon stopped sending purchase orders for the manufacturer's most popular color but continued to buy the slower-selling colors. No matter how many times the manufacturer reached out to Vendor Support, there were no real responses as to why this decision was made. The vendor estimated that he lost more than $250,000 in one year of sales.

These stories bring up many questions, none of them with answers that are clear or obvious from outside of Amazon. Unfortunately, most vendors do not have close relationships with buyers or support personnel inside the Amazon retail operation. They send emails and open online support cases in vain, with most of their communications going unanswered. This one-sided relationship puts many 1P vendors in a completely subordinate role, rather than the kind of partnership one might expect between a vendor and retailer.

Choosing between 3P and 1P

For the vast majority of sellers, third-party selling offers better brand control and opportunities for revenue growth on Amazon. The most compelling reason to choose the 3P option is clear: pricing. In the vendor program, Amazon may squeeze margins, and vendors have little to no recourse. Vendors can request price increases, but these are typically rejected—automatically—when submitted. It can take rounds of appeals and arguments to get even a nominal increase. With inflation, rising labor costs, and more, there is no time to waste.

In addition, 3P sellers have the option to launch new products whenever they wish. On the 1P side, brands are often put in the position of begging Amazon to buy a hot new seller, even if it's the best product out there.

Selling 3P does require additional infrastructure and personnel, as well as skills around inventory management, optimization, and advertising. If the goal is to control the ultimate destiny of the brand, leverage the strength and ubiquity of the Amazon platform—without being dependent on Amazon for purchase orders.

But I'm Already in 1P—Help!

It is possible to rescue your brand from the ravages of Amazon's Vendor program. Many brands have taken this step because they are:

- Hammered by downward pricing pressure
- Unable to offer product variations they know would be successful
- Frequent victims of Amazon stock-outs and lost sales
- Unsupported by promotions and marketing efforts
- Beaten down by the Amazon warehouse, which confuses product variations, fulfills orders incorrectly, receives inbound shipments slowly and inaccurately, and loses or damages large quantities of inventory
- Nickeled-and-dimed by mandatory co-op fees, return fees, transportation fees, and more

Many vendors have never had a third-party selling account. They were recruited by Amazon for the power and attractiveness of their brands. Others were once third-party sellers, but they transitioned to vendor accounts in hopes of an easier, smoother, and more profitable experience on Amazon.

For many brands, there is a better way: Either transition exclusively to a third-party seller account, or sell with a so-called hybrid combination of a third-party account and a vendor account. By going direct to the consumer, with the Amazon Marketplace as a hands-off middleman rather than via a wholesale relationship, companies can benefit from higher margins and better control of their catalog of products.

By moving at least some listings to a third-party selling account, vendors can reap incredible benefits:

- Control of their own pricing. MAP won't be violated, and margins can be protected.
- Ability to list all product variations, which greatly enhances revenue potential.
- Creation of new listings with multi-packs and variety packs. This can result in much higher margins, since consumers will pay a premium, while pick-and-pack fees are lower per quantity sold.
- Control over promotions and pay-per-click ads to drive additional demand.
- Ability to edit and enhance listings that were neglected by Amazon Vendor account managers.

The caveat: Be very careful if you choose a hybrid approach where some items are sold via 1P and others via 3P. Amazon does not allow individual products to be sold on both your 1P and 3P accounts. No mixing and matching is tolerated.

Chapter 3 Summary

- The Amazon third-party Marketplace (3P) offers more long-term flexibility than selling as a 1P vendor.
- 3P sellers control their pricing and product selection, as well as how their goods are advertised and marketed on Amazon. 3P sellers don't need "permission" from Amazon to launch new products, either.
- Amazon recruits vendors by invitation only. Once in the vendor program, these brands lose control over their product selection and pricing on Amazon.

What about you?

1. Do you have products that fit the vendor model? These might include large or heavy items.
2. If your products are not large or heavy, are you willing to provide customer service and take responsibility for your sales? This would lead toward a 3P model for your business.
3. Does your business have an existing vendor relationship with Amazon that would make it difficult to sell 3P? Is it worth transitioning to 3P for potentially better margins and control?

CHAPTER 4

Choose a 3P Business Model That Works for You

In the last chapter, I tried to persuade you to choose a 3P seller account over the 1P vendor model. If I was successful, it's time to dig deeper on the 3P side. Should you be a reseller, a private-label seller with your own branded goods, or something else?

Let's get down to the nitty-gritty of various Amazon business models. Based on what kind of seller avatar most excited you in Chapter 2, you can begin to choose what business model is the best to meet your goals, your risk profile, and your personality.

The basics of Amazon are the same for every seller. Source the product. List the product. Receive orders. Fulfill orders. Get paid. Each seller and each brand have different goals, opportunities, resources, and weaknesses. The way that someone chooses to sell on Amazon should take all of that into account, plus the inherent advantages and disadvantages of the platform itself.

There are as many methods of selling on Amazon as there are Amazon sellers. Let's review the top ways folks sell, and why. In addition, we'll grade each method for its long-term viability, financial performance, and risk.

Reselling Products

Reselling on Amazon is exactly what it sounds like. Companies purchase goods that they turn around and flip to Amazon customers. The avatars most likely to jump on the reseller bandwagon are the Side Hustler and the Classic Entrepreneur. These sellers tend to be product agnostic and focus on sheer supply and demand to choose products they wish to sell.

Buying Products from Wholesalers and Distributors

This is where old-school meets e-commerce. Sellers who specialize in a category, such as sporting goods or beauty, often purchase goods from wholesalers and distributors. Most wholesalers and distributors first qualify the companies that want to offer their products. If the purchasing company passes muster, they receive a catalog of goods from which to choose.

This is where it gets challenging. The purchasing company must choose which items to resell on Amazon. There's a detailed calculus involved. It includes demand for the product, whether it's already an established seller on Amazon, how many other resellers are offering the product already, and what the potential margins might be. Most wholesalers and distributors require a minimum order, which could be any-where from $500 and up. A typical minimum is $1,500 or so. In addition, shipping fees can be expensive.

If you choose to source goods this way, plan to spend large amounts of time researching product catalogs. First, make sure you are allowed to list the items you choose on Amazon. Create a test listing and see if Amazon asks for an application or invoices. You don't want to buy products, only to discover that Amazon will not allow you to list them! (Delete test list-ings for items you do not actually sell.)

Place an order for small quantities of many products, if possible, so you can list them on Amazon and test the waters before investing a large sum on any single item. Pro tip: Make sure the goods you're purchasing from a wholesaler or distrib-utor are eligible for sale online. If they aren't, the resulting conflict can cause heartburn and big money losses.

Long-term viability: Medium. Resellers in this category must always be evaluating their offerings and looking for new and better ones. Winners who sell wholesale get creative by designing product bundles or otherwise differentiating their offerings.

Financial performance: Low margins, high potential vol-ume. This model typically requires a large number of products available on Amazon at any given time. Most likely, these will be low margin since there will be multiple competitors on each listing.

Risk: Low. Sellers should carefully vet their wholesalers and distributors to ensure they have a good chain of cus-tody for their products. As long as that process is thorough, the products are authentic and invoices are strong, this is a low-risk model for sellers. The most common risk is overbuying inventory that cannot be sold quickly enough or for a profitable price.

Retail Arbitrage and Online Arbitrage

Retail arbitrage (RA) and online arbitrage (OA) have launched thousands of businesses on Amazon. The concept is simple. Sellers go to retail stores or visit online retailers. They purchase products that they can flip on Amazon and still make a profit after paying all the relevant selling fees. This is the easiest and fastest way to get up and running on Amazon:

- There are low barriers to entry and low investment required.
- If items are hot, sellers benefit from fast return-on-investment.
- Sellers can capitalize on trends and popular products, like trendy Christmas toys.
- It's a fast way to make a buck.
- Consistency is not necessarily required, making RA and OA a great side-hustle.

However, RA and OA carry their own specific set of risks. Here are some common scenarios:

- Amazon asks for invoices proving a product's authenticity, only to refuse RA or OA receipts. For example, one seller might have a Walmart.com invoice accepted, while another does not.

- Amazon complains because long receipts sent in to prove a product's authenticity are photographed, scanned, or cut.
- OA suppliers don't provide invoices in the format Amazon requires.
- RA and OA items garner intellectual property complaints from brand owners—both valid and invalid—which get sellers in trouble.
- Branded items purchased via RA or OA are suddenly "gated," which happens when Amazon says a seller cannot sell products in a certain category or brand. This leaves the seller with excess inventory and no way to off-load it or recoup costs.
- RA and OA items may have been shelf pulls or customer returns, and customers rightly believe they were old, damaged, or used.

Are You a Bob or a Gary?

Consider two sellers. Bob has all his eggs in the Amazon basket. He recently quit his job to sell on Amazon full-time, and he's focused solely on retail and online arbitrage. Bob spends his time scooping up popular items at large retail chains, dollar stores, and closeout warehouses. If his account were to be suspended, Bob would find himself with no income to support his family.

Gary has a diversified portfolio of income streams. He sells from a brick-and-mortar store. His two Amazon selling accounts feature completely different items: one focuses on hot toys found at retail stores, while the other carries only private-label goods. Gary recently launched a Shopify store, and he already sells on eBay and Etsy.

Which seller is likely to be more concerned about the risks of retail arbitrage? Or, conversely, which seller needs retail arbitrage more to achieve his financial goals?

There are no right or wrong answers here. What if Gary's profitability hinges on his RA toys? What if Bob has tried multiple times to break into wholesale and private label, but has not yet been successful?

Each seller must think through their own risk profile when deciding whether to pursue RA and OA as sourcing strategies. Consider each of the points below, and your risk tolerance for retail and online arbitrage will become clearer:

Certain categories present higher risks for RA/OA sellers. Amazon is cracking down on specific categories that are at higher risk of inauthentic items being sold. Beauty and electronics immediately spring to mind.

Some brands present higher risks as well. The more luxurious or expensive the brand, the more likely a customer will make a counterfeit claim, and RA/OA receipts may not cut it with Amazon.

Some RA/OA sources are more legit than others. Amazon is more likely to accept receipts and invoices from retailers with solid chains of custody for their merchandise. For example, Walmart and Target tend to have strong direct relationships with manufacturers, and their distributors are expected to provide only authentic goods. In contrast, discounters like TJ Maxx and Marshalls buy liquidation deals. There is no proof of the chain of custody for these items. (Think Coach handbags at a discounter—are you sure they are real? Will Amazon believe they are real?) This even applies to your favorite drugstore chains. CVS, Walgreens, and Rite Aid score those awesome endcap deals from liquidators, so the chain of custody is unreliable.

RA/OA items can be shelf pulls and customer returns. A well-known footwear chain fills its online orders by having its brick-and-mortar stores ship items to the customer from right off the sales racks. Often, these shoes are mailed out in clear plastic bags and taped together— no box and no tags included. How many times were those shoes tried on? Do they have paper in the toes to help maintain shape and quality? Other large retailers have similar policies. Even if items ship from the warehouse, some of the stock may be shelf pulls that were used and returned by customers, sometimes in damaged condition.

Is Amazon your only stream of income? If Amazon is the only way you replenish your personal bank account, minimizing risks probably makes sense.

If You're Married to RA, with No Plans for Divorce . . .

Some sellers feel the rewards of RA/OA greatly outweigh the risks. The margins can be excellent, and inventory turnaround can be rapid. It's also a great way for new sellers to enter the world of Amazon sales. If you're one of these folks, consider the following suggestions:

Choose retailers that eschew liquidation. You need to buy brand-new merchandise, not secondhand liquidation lots.

Pick retail sources that Amazon is likely to see as its equal. Amazon gives credit to the big boys. It is unimpressed by dollar stores and their poor discount cousins.

Inspect, inspect, inspect. Even high-end retailers accept returns and then put them back on the floor. Make sure the coffee maker is coffee-free, the curling iron is hair-free, and the cosmetics are sealed.

Choose brands and categories that are less likely to raise eyebrows. Yes, that high-end scarf may have great margins. But without an airtight chain of custody, is it really worth risking your account?

Understand Amazon's condition guidelines. Shelf wear matters. Amazon customers expect items to be brand-new and defect-free. Even a bumped package can spell trouble.

Build multiple streams of income. Sell on other platforms. Create an approved second Amazon account for your private-label offerings. Flip houses. Develop a service business. Do something to ensure you will still have revenue if Amazon takes out your seller account.

Long-term viability: Low. Most RA and OA sellers use this method as a side-hustle or to fund their entry into other ways of online selling. It's physically hard work, with low instances of repetitive products that can be sold long-term. Some of these "replenishables," as they are called in the industry, may last a few months but eventually dry up.

Financial performance: Low to medium margins, with sales volume limited to time and energy of the seller. Sometimes RA and OA products experience margin squeeze, while other products will offer huge winning short-term margins.

Risk: High. Brands file intellectual property complaints with Amazon against OA and RA sellers. A lack of invoices makes proving authenticity difficult. This risk can be somewhat offset by buying at "company stores," such as those in outlet malls, but margins there may not be high enough to sustain a business long-term.

Brand Exclusivity, the Most Exciting Way to Resell

It's one thing to compete against countless other sellers who source products via wholesale, distributors, RA, or OA. It's another thing completely to have an exclusive on Amazon for a brand or a product.

This selling model works for Lifestyle Impresarios, Classic Entrepreneurs, and even some Side Hustlers. Skilled sellers court quality brands and convince them to allow the resale of their product—only by that seller. Any other wholesale purchasers are prohibited from selling the item online.

The seller must first sell their skills to the brand in question, convincing them to essentially outsource their Amazon presence to a single reseller. In return, the seller sets up the Amazon listing page, takes exciting photos, creates Enhanced Brand Content (a.k.a., A+ Content), advertises the product and works to make it successful on Amazon. Exclusive Amazon-only packaging or Amazon-only bundles are a great option in these situations, to keep competitors off the listings. Can it be difficult to find these kinds of exclusive deals? Yes. But a search through business parks and industrial areas of just about any metro area will yield companies with marketable goods that aren't currently being sold online, or at least not on Amazon.

Long-term viability: High. Keep the brand owners happy and add more brands over time. This model can provide income for years.

Financial performance: Medium margins and potentially medium to high volume. As more products and brands are added, the money gets better and better.

Risk: Low. Most brands will negotiate favorable margins, low order minimums and lenient return policies for a reseller doing all the hard work on Amazon to present and protect their image.

Liquidation and the Fast-Track to Destruction. Online auction lots. Truckloads marked for disposal. Salvage stores.

Every Amazon reseller has been tempted by the siren song of liquidation inventory. It's enticing and cheap. Many experts in the Amazon space excitedly tell their social media audiences about the killing they made on auction inventory or lots of overstocks. "After all," they point out with dollar signs dancing in their eyes, "Amazon doesn't say anything in terms of service about liquidation inventory. It's totally OK!"

It's true. Amazon does not specifically address liquidation inventory in its Business Solutions Agreement (BSA), which is the equivalent of most websites' Terms of Service. Amazon also doesn't mention the dangers of liquidation anywhere in its online Help section for sellers. But that doesn't make liquidation an acceptable source of inventory. Liquidation inventory is extremely dangerous for third-party sellers. There is so much that can go wrong. In fact, things could go so wrong that you lose your Amazon seller account permanently.

A little common sense will tell you that liquidation carries elevated levels of risk. Consider these:

- In almost all cases, it's impossible to prove the chain of custody for the products. In other words, you cannot show it is authentic if asked for invoices, or if you field an intellectual property complaint. It takes just one customer complaint saying the item is "fake" for Amazon to request invoices that just don't exist in the right format.
- The products might be counterfeit. Some of the most popular sources of liquidation inventory are Amazon fulfillment centers. Amazon liquidates out products that are slow-movers, overstock, or suspended from the platform. But much of this inventory comes from third-party sellers, and some of it is outright fake.
- Liquidation items are often store returns. They've been opened, used, or refused because they don't work. Even if you have a great inspection process in place, these pieces are only fit for resale as used, or at best, in "open-box" condition.
- Shelf wear has taken a toll. Inventory on the secondary market has been through the wars. It has traveled to multiple warehouses, stores, and customers. Boxes are worn, torn, faded, discolored and dirty. It often just doesn't look new.

Here are some real-world realities from sellers I've helped:

- **Wow, it's from Woot!** A large private-label seller decided to expand his Amazon catalog. He purchased a large lot of Amazon FC liquidation inventory via Woot!, an online store. Almost immediately, he was hit with a slew of intellectual property complaints that were filed with Amazon—more than 100! He was accused of violating the trademarks of others, just by reselling their products. Because these products were purchased at liquidation, the seller could not prove they were authentic. The vast majority of the brand owners refused to retract the complaints they made to Amazon, and the seller's account was deactivated. (You know Woot! is owned by Amazon, right?)

- **PayPal and invoices.** We worked with a relatively new seller who found a load of near-new, name-brand phone cases and accessories. They were from a chain of convenience stores that was closing. When Amazon demanded invoices, he could only show PayPal confirmations for the payment he made to the convenience store owner. There were no detailed invoices with a description of the merchandise purchased. Amazon deactivated his account.

- **Wrecked by returns.** An experienced, longtime seller bought closeout housewares from an auction company, which sourced the items from big-box retailers. The seller inspected the boxes and saw they were sealed, so he sent the inventory to FBA. When the coffee makers he had purchased were sold to Amazon customers, they reported finding moldy coffee inside. Clearly, these were returns that had been re-sealed at the warehouse of the big-box retailer. The seller's account was suspended.

Should you ever purchase liquidation inventory? Here's the seemingly contrary answer: Maybe. It all depends on your personal risk profile—and the risk profile of your business. Many sellers move liquidation inventory quite successfully. If you're determined to sell liquidation, it's important to know the risks. In addition, take the steps to mitigate that risk whenever possible:

Liquidation direct from the manufacturer? Yes, please! Some manufacturers choose to liquidate the last of the inventory in their warehouse when they change packaging or discontinue an item. This kind of purchase can be a relatively safe gold mine, as long as you are listing against the correct version of the product on Amazon.

Be reasonable in your sourcing. Ask yourself: How trustworthy is the chain of custody for these items? For example, a recent client purchased liquidation inventory from a large liquidator that buys directly from big-box chains and has the invoices to prove it. Clearly, this carries less risk than buying from a no-name liquidator on eBay.

Perform serious quality inspections. Liquidation inventory cannot simply be stickered and shipped to FBA. Plus, your team must research to ensure you understand what the items were supposed to look like, what pieces and parts are included, whether the original box had seals, etc.

Adjust your ideas about condition. Conservative is the way to go. If it is even possible that an item was opened, don't grade it as "new."

Put a lot of thought into brand choices. Intellectual property complaints abound on the Amazon platform. Certain brands carry much higher risk than others. It makes sense to stay away from liquidation inventory for premium brands and high-dollar items. In addition, many consumer electronics items would make more sense in the Renewed (certified refurbished) program.

Long-term viability: Low. Most liquidation lots are random products mixed together. A few will be winners. Most will be junk. Product research and grading can be back-breaking work, and it results in a lot of wasted time, money, and energy.

Financial performance: Medium to high margins on the few products that are sellable. But most goods will be too beat up to sell "new," or don't have the margins that make sense for listing goods. Do you really want to spend your time selling the losers at flea markets?

Risk: High. Brands file intellectual property complaints against liquidation sellers. A lack of invoices makes proving authenticity difficult. Bad product condition leads to a lot of complaints.

Drop Shipping—the Right Way

Drop-shipping can be a dream on Amazon. Or it can be a nightmare. In most cases, drop-shipping turns into nightmare fuel. Why? Quacks and self-proclaimed gurus push get-rich-quick drop-shipping schemes that can lead to lost seller accounts and even bankruptcy.

First, a drop-shipping primer. Drop-shipping is a fulfillment method where a third-party seller never sees nor touches the inventory. The third-party seller accepts an order from a customer, and then it triggers another company to fulfill the order.

Amazon allows certain kinds of drop-shipping. A third-party seller can establish a relationship with a vendor such as a manufacturer or distributor. That manufacturer or distributor can then drop-ship on behalf of the third-party seller. Amazon is totally cool with this arrangement, as long as your shipping statistics remain in the green.

But there is another kind of drop-shipping that is specifically prohibited by Amazon. This is casual drop-shipping, where no real vendor relationship exists between the third-party seller and the shipper. For example, a seller may fulfill an order by shipping an item from Home Depot, Walmart, or another Amazon seller direct to the buyer.

There are several reasons informal drop-shipping is dangerous. The item usually arrives in a branded box that isn't from Amazon. This makes customers unhappy. The item typically includes an invoice with the actual price paid to the other online retailer. This makes customers angry since they probably paid much more than that amount. The seller has absolutely no way of controlling product quality. Amazon expects you to ensure that the items you sell meet its stringent product quality standards. If you never see the inventory and have no formal relationship with the vendor, you have no say in quality. Larger items are often shipped without an outer carton. Shipping stickers are placed directly on the box, which is beaten up by the time it arrives. This does not live up to Amazon's standards for third-party sellers.

What happens to retail drop-shippers on Amazon? The consequences can be drastic:

- The seller account may receive a warning (or may not).
- The seller account is suspended.
- The platform permanently holds any funds currently in the account.
- In extreme cases, if funds were recently transferred to the seller, Amazon may claw back funds from the seller's financial institution.

What about drop-shipping the right way? Drop-shipping with formal vendor arrangements can be an excellent sourcing method for some sellers. But just like anything else, it requires careful management and monitoring. This makes the "good" drop-shipping model ideal for Classic Entrepreneurs, who tend to focus a great deal on processes and vendor relationships:

- Have a discussion with your vendor about product quality. Ensure they are only sending your customers items in gift-giving condition.
- Find out about your vendor's packing protocols. If items need to be in a box, make sure they aren't being shipped out in a padded envelope.
- Establish rules for fulfillment times. Carefully monitor your orders and make sure they are going out on time, every time.
- Require timely uploading of tracking numbers for every shipment.

- Whenever possible, automate the entire process, from order transmission to tracking number upload. This greatly reduces human error.

Long-term viability: Medium to high. This depends almost completely on the quality of the drop-shipper, how well they pick-and-pack orders, and if they deliver on time. Find a solid drop-shipper, and you've found a sustainable business model.

Financial performance: Low margins but potentially high volume. On the positive side, the seller doesn't store the inventory—or even touch it. This leads to very low margins. But with enough products listed and marketed well on Amazon, high volume can create a healthy revenue stream.

Risk: Medium. Again, this depends almost exclusively on the quality of the drop-shipper. If they make mistakes, it hurts the seller's account on Amazon. If they do great work, it helps the seller's account on Amazon.

Selling a Brand / Private Label on Amazon

Over the long haul, this is the most profitable and exciting way to sell products on Amazon. It can take a few different forms, each of them attractive and interesting in its own way.

Launching Amazon-Only Products as a Small Private-Label Seller

Welcome to the promised land for Brand Builders and Lifestyle Impresarios, as well as some Classic Entrepreneurs.

I've met a lot of Amazon millionaires who used this model to amass their fortunes. Some grew brands on Amazon and sold them off to an Amazon aggregator, private equity firm, or consumer goods company. This guaranteed their long-term financial future. Many of these folks then took a small portion of their earnings to launch yet another brand and start the process all over again. Others choose to manage and grow their brands over time, eventually creating a healthy stream of income to fund their lifestyles.

This style of Amazon selling requires all the qualities of a traditional business: creativity in product development and design, manufacturing through an outsource, quality control, brand and product marketing, warehousing and storage, order fulfillment, finance, and accounting, and more. Just as with the other styles of selling, Amazon can be chosen as an outsource for warehousing, order fulfillment, and customer service via the FBA program.

Many sellers who choose this arena have a particular affinity for the products they sell. They built a better mousetrap than what's available on the market today. Other sellers simply pursue what they believe can make money. By launching their brands on Amazon, these sellers have a massive national market to test their products. Plus, they can launch immediately, without having to convince a corporate buyer to put their product on retail store shelves.

For example, one seller created a unique product for gun owners. There were no competitors on Amazon.com. He worked with a factory to create a test run and shipped the items to the Amazon fulfillment center. After some advertising and promotional efforts, the product sold out in just a few weeks. The seller continues to scale his business today. He has created variations to the original product, which he also sells on Amazon. In addition, he's branched out into more product ideas for sportsmen.

Long-term viability: Medium to high. Develop a winning product at a fair price, and you've got a long-term business. Competition will be high on Amazon over time, so even the best product cannot rest on its laurels.

Financial performance: Average to excellent margins and any range of sales volume.

Risk: Medium. Again, this depends on whether the products being launched are winners.

Taking Established Products to the Amazon Platform

Some established brands have avoided Amazon like the plague. They believe it's impossible to be successful on the Marketplace and prefer to simply stay away. This is a mistake that leaves money on the table—which is the secret every Corporate Growth Hacker and Big Brand Product Launcher knows.

Even if a brand chooses not to list their goods, their products eventually show up on Amazon anyway. Third-party resellers scoop up inventory from a wholesaler or at a retail store, and they flip it. Unfortunately, they create listing detail pages that are ugly and not representative of the brand.

Brands can choose from a few options:

- They can only control the look and feel of their listings on Amazon. Using Amazon Brand Registry (more on this in a later chapter), the brand can ensure that its preferred images, text, and other details are used on

the pages that promote their products. In addition, they can use Amazon Brand Registry to remove counterfeit offers from the Marketplace.
- Brands can set up 3P accounts and sell their own goods.
- Brands can create Amazon-only offers, such as bundles or items with special packaging. This can keep other sellers off their listings since the items being sold are not available via other sales channels.

What is the downside for brands? Selling on Amazon requires a dedicated team that understands how the Marketplace works. While other platforms can be somewhat easy to navigate, Amazon demands expertise—in advertising, listing page content, inbound shipping to FBA, inventory management, and a whole lot more. Staffing for Amazon takes time and money. But will it pay off? Yes. If they are not in the world's largest marketplace, brands are missing out.

Long-term viability: High. The product is already built. This is simply an expansion to another sales channel.

Financial performance: Good. If the product already has reasonable margins, any dip in profitability due to high Amazon fees should be offset by the benefits of high-volume sales.

Risk: Low. Learn Amazon's rules, play by the book, and all is well.

The Brand Management Route—Private Label Selling without the Hassles

Some brands—large and small—reasonably do not want to develop the core competencies needed to sell on Amazon. They outsource some or all of these functions to agencies.

Full-service Amazon agencies can handle a wide range of services, from listing products to inventory management to advertising and more. Smaller specialty firms may offer just one or two of these. Generally, full-service Amazon agencies charge a flat monthly rate plus a percentage of sales—a kind of "success fee." Each brand must perform its own calculus to determine which is the best financial model for them—handling Amazon in-house or hiring an agency to sweat the details.

Long-term viability: High. The product is already built. This is simply an expansion to another sales channel.

Financial performance: Good. If the product already has reasonable margins, any dip in profitability due to high Amazon fees and agency fees should be offset by the benefits of high-volume sales.

Risk: Low. Learn Amazon's rules, play by the book, and all is well.

Make Your Website Ship Faster with Amazon Buy with Prime

What if you already have an active, e-commerce–enabled website for your brand? Does Amazon have options for you to grow online—without selling directly on the Amazon.com site?

Amazon Buy with Prime enables online stores to leverage Amazon's checkout, Prime delivery service, and returns. The potential benefits for brands and online stores are obvious and attractive. But the likely costs, both financial and otherwise, could be prohibitive for all but the smallest online stores.

Amazon has a sales pitch that starts with its buyers:

- Prime members can shop at online stores (other than Amazon).
- They get fast, free Prime delivery.
- Checkout is seamless and familiar.
- Eligible orders have simple, free returns.
- Shipping and delivery notifications are familiar and prompt.

For sellers, the potential benefits are clear. Amazon's hundreds of millions of Prime members are more likely to buy a product on the seller's website if Prime shipping and returns are included. In addition, sellers outsource pick-pack-and-ship to Fulfillment by Amazon, creating efficiencies for online stores that don't have high-quality, fast fulfillment operations.

For merchants already using FBA, Buy with Prime can be added to their online store within minutes because their inventory is already housed in Amazon fulfillment centers. To get started, merchants:

- Sign up for Buy with Prime.
- Link an Amazon Seller Central account.
- Use Amazon Multi-Channel Fulfillment to offer one pool of inventory for multiple channels.
- Link an Amazon Pay account to offer a seamless checkout experience for Prime members.
- Install a JavaScript widget in their online store to add Buy with Prime to one or more products.

Unlike transactions on Amazon.com, merchants receive shopper order information including email addresses for customer orders, which they can use to provide customer service and build direct relationships with shoppers. In other words, both Amazon and the seller own buyer information. This is a departure from the experience of third-party sellers on Amazon, who most definitely do not own buyer information and are forbidden to use customer details by Amazon's Business Solutions Agreement.

Like any Amazon program, Buy with Prime has some red flags that might not immediately be apparent to merchants without experience selling on the platform. First and foremost are the costs. The full slate of expenses includes unit-based service fees, payment processing fees, fulfillment fees, and storage fees. Just as they do for third-party sellers, the fees are based on product dimensions and weight, average selling price, and number of units per order. There are no subscription fees or long-term contracts. Merchants can expand their inventory and selection at any time, and they can cancel at will.

On the flip side, a merchant may choose to fulfill its orders with a third-party logistics firm instead of with Amazon FBA. A 3PL can store inventory, ship orders, and handle returns for a brand. Or, the merchant may ship orders using its own personnel.

How do Amazon fees compare to an in-house fulfillment operation or a 3PL? That depends. For smaller merchants, Amazon's fees likely will be quite attractive. Smaller sellers have difficulty negotiating favorable shipping rates for two-day delivery. In addition, Amazon's FBA services eliminate the need for warehousing of the inventory in question, as well as the personnel and materials needed to ship orders.

For larger merchants, Amazon FBA can cost more than developing an in-house shipping operation or working with a 3PL. In the worst-case scenario, the fees are comparable when fulfilling orders at scale.

But here's the real difference between FBA and self-fulfillment or a 3PL: accountability. In a nutshell, the Amazon FBA program is completely unaccountable to sellers. Order shipped and delivered late? Too bad. Inventory lost or damaged? You have to file a case and fight to be reimbursed. Weight and dimensions wrong, causing inflated fees? It will probably take an executive escalation to solve. FBA lost your inventory, reimbursed you, and then decided to sell the found units on Amazon Warehouse Deals? Or sold the items to a liquidator? Suck it up. You aren't allowed to control your distribution anymore.

In other words, merchants that embrace Buy with Prime need to know the truth. This is not a "set it and forget it" endeavor, any more than selling as a 3P or Amazon Vendor. And unlike in-house shipping departments or 3PLs, merchants do not have direct recourse when mistakes inevitably occur.

Merchants that ultimately are successful with this program must install a program manager or hire an outside service provider to oversee it.

- Do not trust that Amazon received your shipment in full. Inbound shipments must be monitored, with claims filed for inventory not received.
- Do not trust that Amazon accounts for your inventory and returns correctly. Claims must be filed consistently from month to month, to ensure that merchants are properly compensated for missing items.

- Do not trust that fulfillment fees are calculated accurately. Fulfillment fees and details must be reviewed to ensure the numbers are correct.

Be ready. Like all Amazon programs, it is a ride of highs and lows.

Long-term viability: Medium. It all depends on whether Amazon continues this model over time.

Financial performance: Medium. Product margins are negatively impacted by high Amazon fees.

Risk: Very low. Amazon's best-in-class order fulfillment and good customer service provide low-risk results for most sellers.

Deal Sites, Gift Cards, and Scams—Oh My!

There is an entire category of Amazon sellers that live off the hustle. In this instance, "hustle" doesn't mean "Hey, he works really hard on his side business." Instead, it refers to small-time cons, scams, and swindles.

These flim-flam artists may not technically be breaking the law. But they are stretching it, at a minimum—and Amazon does not approve. If it's too good to be true, it's not a strong foundation on which to grow a business.

For example, there are dozens of Amazon "deal sites" across the internet. Deal sites and their cousins, rebate sites, are not for the convenience or happiness of the Amazon customer. These sites exist to help private-label sellers launch their products on Amazon. They are also used to increase Amazon Best Seller Rank (BSR) or gain Amazon product reviews.

There is an unspoken agreement between these sellers and the deal site customers. Most of the customers on deal sites understand that a product review is expected in return for the steep discount. When sales are made and reviews posted, a product's Best Seller Rank rises. This, in turn, helps the product pop up higher in organic search results.

In most cases, the sellers using these deal sites are offering significant discounts—so much that they are violating Amazon policies against Platform Manipulation. As a result of these discounts, the sellers are losing money on sales made via the discount sites. In return, they hope to drive more buyers to their products.

Some sellers looking for quick flips have chosen to buy products from these deal sites, and then flip them for full price on Amazon.com. Oh, my. If there's any lesson we should all know by now, it's don't scam a scammer. The bad-actor sellers using deal sites have no qualms about reporting folks who flip their goods. They will file fake counterfeit claims with Amazon, and worse. It's not worth the hassle for a few extra bucks. Don't do it.

The same goes for gift card strategies. Sellers obtain discounted Amazon gift cards and use them to buy inventory. But Amazon doesn't exist to allow wheeler-dealers to flip stuff. They want third-party sellers to operate like legitimate businesses, with excellent recordkeeping and reasonable standards for invoices, payments, bank accounts, etc.

- Gift cards can be used for money laundering. This makes them very unattractive to Amazon.

- Gift card discount sites offer cards sourced from members of the public. There is no way to ensure the validity of the cards, nor their provenance.
- When products are purchased with gift cards rather than via a bank account or credit card, the seller cannot provide proof of purchase.

Instead of risking a seller account for a 2 percent to 3 percent discount, look for other ways to game the system. Perhaps the best of these options is to purchase inventory with a debit card or credit card that offers rewards. Some business accounts provide 1 percent or more cash back. Others offer points for travel rewards, merchandise and more.

Long-term viability: Very low. These strategies work until they don't.

Financial performance: Low. Playing around the margins doesn't pay off financially.

Risk: Very high. Once Amazon or the brand catches on, it's game over.

Well, That Was a Lot of Information!

The most valuable thing to take away from this chapter? There are many ways to sell on Amazon. And for most businesses, the best choice is diversity. With diversity, sellers can lower their risks and ensure that they always have one sales channel performing and delivering revenue. Diversity can mean:

- Selling on Amazon and on other platforms and marketplaces

- Selling on Amazon as a private-label brand owner while also selling products wholesale
- Selling as an RA/OA seller while developing and testing your own product line

The possibilities are many. Build one. Then build another. And another. Multiple streams of revenue—both on and off Amazon—provide the best opportunities for long-term wealth and stability.

Chapter 4 Summary

- 3P sellers have many options on the Marketplace. Resellers might source their products from wholesalers, distributors, liquidators, or directly from brands. Each of these strategies carries different risks and potential profitability.
- Brands and private-label sellers have the greatest long-term potential for stability and success on the Amazon platform.
- Avoid risky models like prohibited drop-shipping, discount gift cards, and liquidation lots. These can stop your Amazon business in its tracks before you even get a chance to really get going.

What about you?

1. Do you have any existing relationships that could create an opportunity to sell items exclusively on Amazon?

2. Are there any special interests you have that might lead you to manufacture a winning private-label product?
3. If you have an existing brand off Amazon, what kind of special packaging or bundle could drive traffic to your Amazon listings without compromising your other sales channels?

Part 2

Set Up Your Amazon Business for Success

CHAPTER 5

Build a Winning Amazon Business Plan

You need a vision. Then you need a plan. In a few simple steps, you can develop both and have a path for future Amazon success.

A traditional long-form business plan may be too daunting for most Amazon and online sellers. And let's face it: a lot of business plan formats are just . . . long. They are granularly detailed and full of information that's not necessary unless you are applying for a business loan or trying to entice a suitor to buy your company. If you're an entrepreneur more focused on hustle than documentation, how about creating a quick bullet-point business plan? Let's get to work!

Start with a Vision for Your Business— and for You

Have you ever seen a truly inspiring vision board? Also known as a dream board or goal board, a vision board is a collage of images, words, and symbols that reflect the future you want to achieve, experience, or manifest in your life. It can be a physical poster board or an electronic document. It might include photos, illustrations, religious verses, quotations, or inspirational words. Affirmations and personal mementos can be a unique extra touch.

To me, there are two purposes to a vision board:

1. It encourages the creator to emotionally connect with their goals and dreams. It's one thing to write out a list of words to express your desired future. It's another to design artwork, translating those words into feelings and innermost longings.

2. It serves as daily reinforcement of your "why." When working hard on the drudgery of the day-to-day, it's so easy to forget why you're investing so much time and energy into your business. A vision board reminds you at a glance of the future you are creating with your efforts. It is positive thinking writ large and available when you most need it.

If someone works to create a vision board that truly represents their deepest desires, it will be as unique as their fingerprint or their DNA. Few people would come up with the same goals and wants for both the short-term and the future.

I'll admit to having been somewhat averse to vision boards—until I created one. As a person with concrete and linear thinking patterns, it's challenging for me to envision audacious material goals. It took practice for me to get into the swing of things and come up with bold ideas for my future. I say this to encourage others who are resistant to the vision board concept: just go with it. Give it a shot. It might just change your view of destiny, for yourself and those you love.

Break out a posterboard, glue, markers, and even the dreaded glitter. Thumb through magazines and travel brochures. Search the internet and print out photos. Create a collage that speaks to your soul, inspires you to work, and gives you a sense of peace with the future.

Work through HARD Goals First

Vision boards can inspire. But they lack the specificity entrepreneurs need. They also tend to focus on material things, and they don't always encourage adventurous goals that are in line with a person's morals, ethics, and spirituality.

To balance the materialism and generality of the vision board, spend a day thinking about your HARD goals. The HARD acronym, which stands for Heartfelt, Animated, Required, and Difficult, was created by Mark Murphy, the CEO of Leadership IQ. This goal-setting framework is geared toward motivation, engagement, and performance:

Heartfelt: HARD goals are emotionally compelling and personally meaningful. They align with your values, passions, and long-term aspirations. By setting heartfelt goals, you tap into your inherent motivation. This creates a sense of purpose that fuels your drive and commitment. In other words, these goals are so close to your reasons for being, they become part of your very soul.

Animated: HARD goals are vivid and inspiring. They paint a clear picture of what success looks like, creating a compelling vision that captures your imagination. You can close your eyes and picture what success would look like.

You can feel the excitement of reaching your goal. This pushes forward creativity and ignites determination. You don't want to stop until you hit the target.

Required: HARD goals are challenging and push you outside of your comfort zone. They require dedication, and a willingness to go above and beyond. Required goals reflect a commitment to growth and excellence. You will have to give everything you've got, but it will be worth it.

Difficult: HARD goals stretch your capabilities and push the boundaries of what you believe is possible. They are ambitious and may seem daunting at first. Difficult goals encourage you to embrace challenges, develop new skills, and persevere in the face of obstacles.

HARD goals are "stretch" goals. They are big and audacious. They push you beyond what you believe you can actually do. They also encourage entrepreneurs to think holistically about their business, and how it can impact their personal life, their family, and causes they care about. It's a goal ecosystem, where everything works together.

Use these examples to get your creative HARD goal juices flowing:

- Replace your income in eighteen months and quit the job you hate
- Fund your kids' college expenses without debt
- Pay off your home mortgage in five years
- Fully fund your investment accounts and create an option for early retirement

- Earn enough money to give generously to your favorite cause, or to start your own not-for-profit organization
- Create products that will change lives or address a specific challenge

Then Tackle SMART Goals

SMART goals are tactical. They are how you can translate your vision board and HARD goals into a day-to-day action plan.

SMART is an acronym that stands for Specific, Measurable, Achievable, Relevant, and Time-bound. It is a framework created by George T. Doran and commonly used in goal setting and project management to ensure that objectives are well-defined and effectively pursued. Each element of the SMART framework represents a critical aspect of a goal that helps make it more meaningful and actionable. Let's break down each component:

Specific. A goal should be clear and well-defined. It should answer the questions of who, what, when, where, and why. By being specific, you provide a clear direction and focus for your efforts.

Measurable. Goals should be quantifiable, allowing you to track progress and determine when they have been successfully achieved. Measurable goals use concrete criteria and indicators to assess their completion.

Achievable. A goal should be realistic and attainable. While it's important to set challenging objectives, they should still be within your capabilities and resources.

Setting overly ambitious goals can lead to frustration and demotivation.

Relevant. Goals should be aligned with your broader objectives and aspirations. They should be meaningful and relevant to your overall purpose or the specific context in which they are set. Goals that are relevant provide a sense of purpose and contribute to your long-term vision.

Time-bound. Goals should have a specific time frame or deadline attached to them. This helps create a sense of urgency and provides a target to work toward. Having a time frame in mind also enables you to break down the goal into smaller milestones and track your progress effectively.

By applying the SMART framework to your goal-setting process, you can enhance focus, and motivation. It encourages you to think critically about your objectives and ensures that they are well-defined, actionable, and aligned with your broader aspirations.

For a new Amazon entrepreneur, sample SMART goals might be:

- Generate $10,000 of revenue in the first month of sales by launching an initial private-label product and ad campaign in the pet category.
- Launch three additional private-label products in the pet category before the end of the year.
- Test different product photos for one item each month, for three months. Based on those findings, improve photos for all your Amazon products.

- Call on ten manufacturers to ask for an Amazon exclusive in the next two months, with the goal of signing deals with two brands.

Get Set Up the Right Way

Goal setting was the hard part. The next step is the most basic. Set up your business—the legitimate way. You will need:

- An LLC to protect you from risk
- An EIN, which is a federal tax number or Employer Identification Number
- A business bank account registered in the name of the LLC
- A business credit card for your Amazon account
- A local or state business license if it is required in your jurisdiction
- Product liability insurance that meets Amazon's requirements

Once you have these documents available, register for a Seller Central account at sellercentral.amazon.com. Amazon will ask for personal and LLC information. Then, they will schedule a time for a verification call. This is a video call where a representative will confirm your documents and that you are a real person. (This process changes from time to time, so don't be shocked if a video call is not required.)

Then, you need a basic accounting system, including a method for tracking all expenses including mileage driven in your vehicle for the business. Don't be put off or daunted by the word "accounting." Thanks to all the technology available today, financial recordkeeping can be easy! Keeping clean books is absolutely critical from day one. At the end of the year, you will have to file a tax return. This requires a list of income and expenses. If you don't log expenses, you can't file an accurate tax return—or you will pay too much in taxes.

Good recordkeeping requires creating a filing system for invoices, payment records, and product documentation. Ideally, these records should be kept electronically so they may be easily searched and found at a moment's notice. Your accountant may need invoices for your books and your tax filings. Amazon may also ask for invoices and other documentation along the way.

Know Your Numbers

Let's face it. Revenue is sexy. YouTube is loaded with videos of retail arbitrage and online arbitrage sellers, showing mountains of goods they sourced and sold. With this come screenshots of their massive revenue increases over time.

"I joined the $1 million club. Look at me!" This is particularly true for Lifestyle Impresarios and Side Hustlers, who are motivated to rack up flashy numbers.

The most obvious number for most new sellers to focus on is revenue. Without sourcing and selling goods, there is no point in an Amazon seller account. Plus, talking about revenue is fun. Top-line growth is always exciting. The close-out that a seller negotiated with a distributor; the hottest toy they swept off every store shelf in a 200-mile radius; the Amazon exclusive they negotiated with a local manufacturer.

But whether the revenue screenshot shows a $100,000-a-month seller or a $10 million-a-month enterprise, it means absolutely nothing if the bottom line is in the red.

The Amazon coaches, programs, and message boards mostly encourage a focus on revenue numbers. They even challenge sellers to share their revenue screenshots to impress their friends and colleagues. Yet few coaches want to dig into the nitty-gritty of profitability. Expenses are both boring and important.

Unfortunately, too many sellers do not know their numbers on the expense side. Direct expenses add up quickly. For each and every product, also known as an ASIN (Amazon Standard Identification Number, pronounced AY-sin), a seller must understand:

- Cost of goods sold (COGS), or what it costs to buy each unit of the ASIN
- Per-unit storage and operating expenses for the seller's own warehouse
- FBA expenses, including pick-and-pack fees, commission, inventory storage fees, etc.
- Prep expenses per unit, which might include shrink wrap, bubble wrap, boxing, stickering, etc.
- Shipping expenses per unit, whether the seller is fulfilling the order themselves or sending it to an Amazon Fulfillment Center (FC)
- Advertising cost of sales (ACOS)

Then come overhead and indirect expenses:

- Transportation (gas, mileage, wear-and-tear—however you calculate it in your business)
- Warehousing
- Salaries
- Utilities
- And so many more

When sourcing products to sell, there is a calculus. Can the selling price be such that it covers all the direct expenses listed above, plus overhead and indirect expenses, and still make a profit? What if there is a race to the bottom on price for some of the goods the seller listed? What if a seller has to significantly mark down inventory to get it out the door? Will it still make a profit?

Why Many Sellers Don't Know Their Numbers

Most Amazon sellers are great at the treasure hunt. Sourcing products is a rush. They aren't so great at recordkeeping. They don't track expenses, and some don't even keep their invoices and receipts organized. Then tax time rolls around. If sellers provide a complete record of all expenses to their accountant, they may be shocked—they may not have made a profit at all. This is particularly true of Side Hustlers, who are pressed for time and working Amazon as a second job. Those pursuing products to flip tend to lose track of receipts and fail to record their mileage. They are much more focused on finding the hottest products.

In addition, the Amazon seller app is focused primarily on inventory and revenue on the Amazon channel. It's not designed to help sellers understand profitability of their individual ASINs, nor the larger picture of how their business is running. Let's face it: avoiding these details benefits Amazon, since showing sellers large expenses and fees doesn't encourage them to add more listings and send more inventory to FBA warehouses.

Too many times, we've heard clients say, "I didn't keep up with my expenses as the months went by. At the end of the year, once my books were closed, I discovered that I was making less than minimum wage." It happens. It happens a lot.

What's a seller to do? Get obsessed about tracking data. All the data, and right from day one:

- COGS on a product-by-product basis
- Direct expenses on a product-by-product basis
- Pricing over time
- PPC by product
- Mileage
- Hours worked
- Everything!

Find good software. There are many options out there for Amazon sellers. Simply enter the ASIN and your COGS, and the software will automatically import data about FBA fees and help estimate other expenses. Then you can understand profitability for individual products. Which should you buy more of? Which should you discontinue? The data reveals it all.

Here's the most important part. Make an appointment with yourself for the first day of the month, every month for the rest of the year. Write it in your appointment book or set an alarm on your phone today! At the appointed time, review the numbers and make sure you stay on track. Don't let one month pass without completing this exercise. It will show you which products are making you money, and which should be discontinued from your catalog.

The Quick-and-Dirty Amazon Business Plan

There's no need to be formal when creating your Amazon business plan. Bullet points will do. Remember, this document is for you and you alone. Based on your vision and your goals, write down the following:

Sources and uses of funds. How much cash do you have available to launch an Amazon business? How do you think that capital is best deployed at the outset—buying inventory, setting up basic infrastructure, hiring part-time help, etc.

Products. What can you do in this arena that nobody else can do? Where do you have unique strengths and opportunities?

Market research for your proposed products. There are a number of excellent and inexpensive tools that can make market research easier and more accurate. These include software such as Jungle Scout and Helium 10, as well as others. You can determine how many competitive products are on Amazon, their monthly sales, price points, listing quality, and more.

Marketing strategy. Again, where are your strengths? Determine where you can outsource important functions such as listing optimization, advertising campaign management, social media, website development, and more. Outline the budget you can access to support these efforts.

Operations. Consider what operational locations you currently have available—ideally at low or no cost. Think about how you plan to fulfill orders and what resources will be needed to do so. What about human capital to pick-and-pack, ship inventory to Amazon FBA, answer customer service messages, and handle the day-to-day of account management?

Using a calendar, write down some realistic deadlines. When will your Amazon account be set up? When will you have your first products sourced and delivered? When will you be ready to tackle ad campaigns?

If you're not ready to answer all the above questions, don't fret! We will review many of these topics in the following chapters, which should assist with brainstorming and decision-making.

Amazon Sellers Need a Disaster Plan

Don't think it cannot happen to you. For small and mid-sized businesses, disasters can take many forms:

- Fires that destroy your home, warehouse, or office
- Tornadoes, hurricanes, earthquakes, and severe storms that damage office and home locations or take out power and communications
- Power or internet outages—from a day to a week—that disrupt your ability to fill orders and communicate with customers
- Personal illness or family emergencies that make owners, managers, or key employees unable to fulfill their work responsibilities

Does it sound far-fetched? It's not. I've worked with sellers whose accounts were suspended because they failed to fulfill merchant-fulfilled orders on time. One woman was abused by her boyfriend and fled to a domestic violence shelter. One man's shop, where he manufactured his own products, was flooded. One business was in a hurricane area, and employees were not allowed to get anywhere near the warehouse for days.

So what's an Amazon business to do? Have a disaster plan in place, and train your entire team on the details. Think through these action steps:

1. Make sure more than one person has the ability to put your Amazon seller account on vacation mode. If a fire, flood, or personal disaster strikes and you cannot fulfill orders, it's critical to go on vacation ASAP while you sort out the details. In vacation mode, you will not receive any merchant-fulfilled orders. Amazon will, however, continue to sell your FBA inventory that is in stock, and it will provide customer service for these orders.

2. Have more than one team member trained to answer customer service messages. Again, in the event orders cannot be filled or are filled late, you must be able to communicate this to customers as soon as possible. By being open and honest, you will avoid negative feedback and unwanted cancellations.

3. Train your team to understand that going on vacation mode to protect your account is more important than ensuring a flow of new orders. Don't let the panic of temporary lost revenue tempt you into making business-ending mistakes.

4. Have a backup location for your inventory. Do you know of a storage space, warehouse, or other solution in case your current location is damaged or off the grid? How would you move your inventory there in a disaster?

5. Create a virtual "fulfillment relocation kit." Know which technology and tools would be needed to replicate your fulfillment operations quickly and easily in another location—such as a laptop, label printer, shrink wrap solution, boxes, labels, etc.

6. If your business operates on platforms other than Amazon, be ready to leverage social media to communicate with your customers. Have canned graphics ready to go, and let your loyal customers know what's going on, how they can help, and when they can expect you to be back in business.

Planning ahead can save you a lot of headaches in the end—and ensure your business is back to creating cash flow faster.

Expanding to Other Marketplaces and Platforms

As mentioned earlier, it makes sense to tackle the Amazon Marketplace first, for many reasons. But in the long run, nobody should keep all their eggs in the Amazon basket. That might mean expanding to Walmart or Etsy, selling excess inventory or returns on eBay, setting up your own website, or selling in physical stores.

From the beginning, keep an open mind about where your products might best be received and successful. Learn about other platforms and talk to sellers about how they have grown businesses past the Amazon marketplace.

Make this part of your Amazon business plan. Never stop thinking about what other options make sense for you.

A Simple, Sample Amazon Plan

Let's follow the methodology in this chapter to create a quick, bullet-pointed plan for an imaginary seller named Dave. Our buddy Dave has worked at corporate jobs for a decade, and he's ready to strike out on his own. With a growing family and financial responsibilities, Dave intends to start his Amazon journey as a Side Hustler. Ultimately, he would like to be a Brand Builder who develops health products and exercise tools for bodybuilders. He created a vision board that featured fun family vacations, no debt or financial stress, and a lifestyle centered on personal well-being.

Dave decided on a simple HARD goal: replace his corporate income in twelve months, so he can quit his job and focus on his Amazon business. To do this, Dave's SMART goals include:

- Launch three new products per quarter.
- Test packaging and advertising strategies with each new launch; propagate winning ideas across future product launches.
- Reinvest all profits in the business for twelve months.
- Use income from his full-time job to pay off $20,000 in credit card debt over twelve months, which will reduce financial pressures once he quits his job.

Dave investigated three possible suppliers who could manufacture his first three product ideas. He ordered sample inventory from each and calculated the exact costs and expenses per unit, including overhead. This enabled him to determine his profit margins over the next year if all goes well.

Dave began working with a friend who creates marketing and branding on a freelance basis. He registered his trademark. He set up an office and warehouse space in his basement. While Dave planned to rely on Amazon FBA, he created a backup plan to ship his own orders if needed. He purchased low-cost equipment and boxes, and he learned how to package his own goods and buy postage.

In a matter of months, Dave was working both his HARD and SMART goals.

Chapter 5 Summary

- Begin with the end in mind. Even the most basic business plan helps a new Amazon seller obtain needed direction, motivation, and deadlines.
- Vision boards, HARD goals, and SMART goals provide needed structure.

- A business plan doesn't have to be complex. Bullet-point your strategy.
- Don't put your business plan in a drawer. Update it over time. It should be a living document that continually points the way.
- Consider what the future may hold, whether it's selling on other channels or in brick-and-mortar stores.

What about you?

1. Break out the scissors and glue! Create a vision board that speaks to your heart and soul. Don't limit yourself to material goals. Describe the lifestyle, spiritual growth, and family you wish to have in the future.

2. Get specific with your goals. Don't be afraid to write down goals just because you may not reach them. You may not, and that's ok! Without goals, however, you have no direction with which to start.

3. Be realistic about the resources you must have to get started, from cash to physical locations to people who may be of assistance. The more detailed you are, the better. This will help you see the "holes" in your resources and seek out ways to fill them.

4. Don't let the perfect be the enemy of the good. Take a step today. Take another step tomorrow. You don't need perfect circumstances or a full-blown strategy for every facet of the business. Fill in your business plan as you go. You can do it!

CHAPTER 6

It's All about the Product

Look how far you've come in your Amazon journey! You've chosen an avatar, decided between 3P and 1P selling, settled on a sourcing method or two, and developed a quickie business plan. What's next? It's time to find a winning product to sell on Amazon.

When you sell on the "everything store," how can your products stand out from the millions of goods already being offered? How can you sell an item that's competitively priced, but still make a profit? Can you move enough volume to generate the cash flow you need? These are key challenges for all Amazon businesses, whether you are a reseller or manage your own brand.

Selling products is important. But sourcing them is critical. Your profit is made at the buy. If you pay too much for goods that cannot command a high enough sales price, you will never be in the black. Keep this in mind as you consider what products you wish to offer.

Generic Items Are a Losing Proposition on Amazon

New sellers are often enticed by the siren song of generic products, which can be easily found in bulk on overseas websites such as Alibaba. Sellers find extremely inexpensive items with no branding, and then they list those products against existing ASINs on Amazon. There are a few problems this can create. Typically, the existing ASIN is branded—rightly or wrongly.

Sellers should avoid selling generic or white box items on Amazon. Amazon will not help you out if you pursue this strategy. Amazon wants everything to be branded. Why? Generic items are nothing but trouble:

- Other sellers get on your listing and sell a different version of the product.
- Other sellers create duplicate listings of your product, and there is nothing you can do about it because your item is not branded.
- Amazon asks for invoices after a customer complaint, and they cannot match a brand name to help them verify the invoice. This can result in your listing or account being shut down.

If you decide to create branding for an item that was previously generic, you must have the brand appear on both the product and the packaging. It must be manufactured under your brand. It's not enough to simply put your sticker on an existing product, and claim it is yours.

Research, Research, Research

No matter how you source inventory, research is critical for any Amazon seller. You must understand the basics:

- Demand. You need products that can sell at least ten units per day. Look for products that are not seasonal since it's better if you can sell items all year long.
- Opportunity. Look for low competition on the individual product listing, or on competitive listings. Strive to find products where you can offer a lower price for the same or better quality than the competition.
- Size. Products that are small and light offer better margins, thanks to lower shipping costs, less storage space, and lower FBA fees.
- Customer satisfaction. Some products are much more likely than others to garner complaints and suffer from high return rates. Clothing has frequent returns for sizing issues, for example. Some goods are difficult to assemble or break frequently. Look for items that are simple to use and unlikely to be returned.
- Legal challenges. Large and high-end brands don't like resellers. They are more likely to file complaints against you, so avoiding them is smart. Other potential areas to avoid are consumables, such as food, supplements, and beauty products.

With all this in mind, it's time to spend time on some serious research. This requires a software tool such as Helium 10 or Jungle Scout. These allow you to explore market demand, competition, and trends. Also take some time to review product reviews, Amazon Best Seller Rank (BSR), and the like.

Learn about keyword research and immerse yourself in the keywords related to the products you wish to offer.

Ideally, look for a niche or gap in the market where you can differentiate your product. Find product categories with high demand, but that are not oversaturated with competition. Or, seek out opportunities to improve existing products or offer unique features.

Once you've found some potentially good sellers:

- Conduct a profitability analysis. Consider the selling price, manufacturing or sourcing costs, shipping fees, Amazon fees, and any other relevant expenses. Calculate the estimated profit margins and ensure they align with your business goals. For example, imagine you wish to sell body lotion. In addition to the cost of the goods, you will need to determine how much it will cost to ship the lotion to your warehouse. Then, figure the cost per tube for either shipping to the Amazon FBA warehouse or to the average customer, including shrink wrap, bubble wrap, boxes, tape, etc.
- Decide whether the product works at Amazon FBA. Do the fees make sense? Does it fall into any expensive categories like Dangerous Goods, which require higher shipping costs and storage fees? For example, body sprays and other personal care items containing alcohol fall under "hazardous materials." They can cost as much as ten times the regular fee to ship to Amazon FBA. Plus, the fulfillment and storage costs are higher.
- Think about branding and differentiating. Whether you are a reseller or a private-label seller, consider how you can differentiate your product and create a unique

brand. Identify ways to add value through packaging, branding, product variations, or bundling. Developing a strong brand and unique selling proposition can help you stand out from competitors.

- Evaluate your supplier. Identify reliable suppliers or manufacturers for the product. Ensure they meet your quality standards, can handle production volume, and offer competitive pricing. Consider factors like lead time, product customization options, and their ability to scale with your business. Don't forget to think about the ease of the relationship. If you needed documentation to send to Amazon, would the supplier help in a timely manner?

- Validate the products. Before committing to a product, conduct a small test order or a trial run to validate its market demand and customer acceptance. This can help you gather real-world feedback and make adjustments before scaling up production or making larger orders. Consider the body lotion we discussed above. Can you order a case of twenty-four units from the supplier, ship it to Amazon, and see how long it takes to sell? Based on performance, you can make a more educated decision about long-term purchases of this item.

Product Quality above All Else

You found the perfect product. Sales rank is stellar. The price is right. The listing has limited competition. What could go wrong? I've got two words for you: product quality.

Amazon is obsessed with buyer experience. A perfect buyer experience is the easiest way to get great product reviews, earn positive store feedback, increase revenue over time, and avoid costly returns. It's also how you stay out of trouble with Amazon itself. The company gets very unhappy when buyers are unhappy, and complaints mostly stem from one thing: product quality.

In years past, Amazon assigned the blame for many product quality problems to manufacturers. Sellers just had to be sure they sold new goods in pretty boxes without dents or dings. That is no longer the case. Amazon now expects sellers to sell quality products that garner as few customer complaints as possible. The proof for this is in the ever-increasing number of ASIN suspensions focused on everything from inauthentic to used items sold as new to safety incidents and more.

Why has Amazon undertaken this strategy?

- Knock-offs. Whether they are from disreputable sellers here in the United States or overseas, inauthentic goods have flooded the Amazon platform. To remain a trusted source for customers, Amazon must combat this influx of fakes whenever possible. Suspending ASINs with inauthentic complaints and demanding invoices as proof of authenticity is happening more than ever.
- Warehouses bulging with cheap Alibaba goods that nobody wants. Amazon has been flooded with poor-quality goods that simply don't sell. The company needs to get those out of their warehouses and out of the catalog. That's one reason Amazon has become

more aggressive with fees and policies for FBA long-term storage.

- Irresponsible sellers. I hate to say it, but it's true. Sellers have shirked their responsibilities. Far too often, a seller has high returns for a poor-quality item, but doesn't act—or even notice.

If you have an ASIN suspended for product quality, does that mean you are selling fakes or acting irresponsibly? Absolutely not! But as most Amazon sellers know, the whole class gets punished for the actions of a few troublemakers. Amazon has ratcheted up enforcement on product quality, and it is now sellers' responsibility to act accordingly.

You can combat product quality problems right at the source. Think about product quality throughout the product sourcing process to avoid items that are badly made, poorly packaged, or won't ship well.

For sourcing:

- Don't just consider margins and sell-through rates. Look at the quality of the product. Read reviews. If there are only three stars and a bunch of unhappy customers on Amazon.com, consider passing on the buy.
- If this is a high-volume wholesale or private-label buy, do more extensive research. Ask about product testing, materials, and more. Don't buy something that might fall apart, break easily, or has poor directions.
- Use the product. Try to break it. Consider how other people of different backgrounds might use and abuse it. This kind of thought process can reveal shortcomings and product quality issues.

For shipping:

- Can your product arrive to the buyer in pristine condition? If not, you have a product quality issue. For example, some pressed-powder cosmetics are in flimsy boxes, leading to breakage. Without upgraded outer packaging, you will have many unhappy customers.
- Is the product packaging zero-movement for items that can be damaged in transport? If you are selling goods that are glass or plastic, they need to be tightly packed into boxes, where they will not move or be crushed.
- Are boxes and bottles adequately sealed? Manufacturers don't love adding safety seals, making this a point of negotiating for private-label sellers. But the expense and trouble of adding safety seals to bottles and boxes pays off in the end, with lower returns and fewer complaints.

The obsession with product quality cannot end when you choose an item to sell. Instead, you must continually monitor to find any problems that arise:

- Run return reports frequently. Hardline items should have return rates of less than 3 percent.
- Check the reasons for returns—even if your return rate is acceptable. Find out why your customers are returning items and what makes them unhappy. Don't ignore these issues. Address them.
- Read product reviews. Yes, there are difficult customers. But even cranky people can provide valuable feedback.

- Assign someone in your company the duty of monitoring, measuring, and acting on this data. Make it part of their weekly responsibilities. Don't let it slide.

Amazon Exclusive Items

The most exciting items to sell on Amazon are exclusive items. There are several ways to create Amazon exclusives:

- Find a small manufacturer or brand owner without an Amazon presence. Manage their Amazon brand in return for exclusivity, meaning you are the only seller for their products on Amazon or online. One seller I know found an automotive accessories manufacturer near his home. For more than three years, he has been offering their briskly selling products on Amazon with no competition. In return, he has created beautiful listings and managed online ads for their brand.
- If you have an established brand, create Amazon-only packaging or bundles. This can protect your distribution and help you control who sells your brand online, and how. For example, a major cleaning products company sold a bundled two-pack of its most popular kitchen spray with a branded microfiber cloth. This way, RA and OA sellers cannot duplicate the bundle and compete on the Amazon listing.
- Resellers can also create bundles if they follow Amazon's detailed bundling rules. Be sure to get educated on the latest standards for bundles before following this course of action.

A Fast-Track to Success: Licensed Products

Buyers love brands that they are familiar with, admire, or desire. Fortunately for Amazon sellers, there are brands up for sale. By paying a licensing fee, you can put a well-known brand on your somewhat generic products—and beat the competition.

For example, a cable network brand was licensed and placed on a line of pet products. Upon launch, these items immediately jumped to the top of the bestsellers list on Amazon. Sellers also license characters from children's programming for T-shirts, bedding, home décor, and much more. The only limit is your imagination.

Licensing is not cheap, nor is it easy. But in the long run, it can be a gold mine:

- Consider products that you can easily access through existing supplier relationships or manufacturers.
- Brainstorm what licenses could create demand for those products. Character-branded clothing and backpacks are an obvious choice that is often successful. But there are no limits to the creativity you can employ.
- Ensure the quality of the products you're offering. High-quality licensors will insist on excellent product quality and consistency.
- Reach out to brands to negotiate. Most brands will let you know their fees right up-front. As in many agreements, you may be able to negotiate a better rate based on volume.
- Calculate the cost per item and ensure you will make a handsome profit.

- Employ the services of a good lawyer, who will finalize the contract and ensure you have an option to renew if your products are successful.

A Lesson from COVID-19: Rethinking the Supply Chain

As US ports began gradually clearing in late 2021 and early 2022, some brand owners began to relax a bit about their recently fraught relationship with the supply chain. They believed that delivery times from their Chinese manufacturers would go back to normal—meaning, timeframes as they were prior to COVID-19.

Unfortunately, continued lockdowns in China kept the supply chain in chaos. Some Chinese manufacturers folded, and a zero-tolerance COVID-19 policy shut down factories and even entire towns seemingly on a whim, with no end in sight. This was all compounded by protests, which could be a factor in the future as well.

That's why many Amazon private-label sellers and other brand owners began looking to other countries—including closer to home—for manufacturing capabilities. Popular choices included India, Mexico, and here in the United States.

When sourcing new products, don't be afraid to think outside of the China box. There are deals to be found with manufacturers in other countries. In addition, Amazon has become stricter about sellers avoiding manufacturers that abuse human rights. Keep this in mind during your sourcing conversations and research.

Chapter 6 Summary

- Research is foundational for Amazon product sourcing. Sellers must understand the demand for their potential products, how many units might sell each week, cost structure, ongoing fees, and more.
- Generic items are not welcome on Amazon. Don't go there.
- On the flip side, Amazon buyers love healthy brands. Licensing deals and bundles with popular branded products are possible options for "exclusive" products that others cannot copy or compete against.

What about you?

1. Check out product research software and choose a subscription. Familiarize yourself with the app and get ready to dive deep.
2. Watch YouTube tutorials and read e-books about the software you choose. Power users and the software companies themselves provide excellent resources to give you a jump start on product research.
3. Create a checklist that you plan to use internally for potential suppliers. Include quality controls, social responsibility, delivery time, and other variables.

CHAPTER 7

The Pros and Cons of FBA

You've settled on the products you'd like to sell. But where are you going to put them? And will you be spending your days running orders to the post office? That's the next set of questions you must answer to launch a successful Amazon business. The answer for most sellers? Amazon FBA.

Amazon FBA is a game-changer. It's the reason that companies have flocked to and invested in the Amazon Marketplace, while avoiding or ignoring other online selling options.

With FBA, the smallest sellers can offer the same shipping speeds and service as Amazon—no massive warehouse or pick-and-pack employees required. In addition, sellers with FBA offers are more likely to qualify for the Buy Box, which is Amazon's preferred offer that it serves up to customers for any given product. Combine these factors, and FBA has become indispensable for thousands of sellers on the Marketplace—and will continue to be in the future.

What Is Amazon FBA?

FBA is Fulfillment by Amazon. FBM is Fulfillment by Merchant, often called "seller fulfilled." At Riverbend Consulting, we serve thousands of sellers. The majority prefer FBA vs. FBM. In fact, our client base mirrors what a report from Jungle Scout revealed: 86 percent of sellers choose FBA, 37 percent are FBM, and 22 percent choose both.[1]

With Amazon FBA, a third-party seller ships inventory to Amazon fulfillment centers (FCs). They may be able to send items to just one FC, or they may have to split their shipment of goods and send it to multiple FCs. Amazon receives the inventory. Then, it breaks the shipment down further, transshipping units to several other FCs. This way, the goods are stored in warehouses that are closer to customers all over the country. Transshipping enables Amazon to meet or beat the two-day Prime shipping promise expected by Prime members. When an order is placed, Amazon warehouse workers pick, pack, and ship the item. In addition, Amazon handles returns and customer service inquiries for FBA inventory.

Choosing between FBA and FBM

So, what should be your fulfillment strategy and why? What makes the most sense financially, logistically, and operationally? Here's more information to help you decide.

---

1 Jungle Scout. "The State of the Amazon Seller." 2023. https://www.junglescout
.com/amazon-seller-report/?utm_medium=johnathanlyman8137&utm
_source=affiliate&pscd=get.junglescout.com&ps_partner_key
=am9obmF0aGFubHltYW44MTM3&ps_xid=2dbWw1XrShpGCj&gsxid
=2dbWw1XrShpGCj&gspk=am9obmF0aGFubHltYW44MTM3

Costs. Amazon fees are no joke. Not only do existing fees keep escalating over time, but new fees are on the upswing. This is a particular hardship for new sellers or those with low-margin products. Ultimately, it means doing the math to determine if FBM is less expensive than FBA's fees-driven approach. In contrast, FBA may be more cost-effective for some sellers. For example, if you're dealing with high-volume sales or have items that are particularly difficult to ship, FBA's economies of scale may make it the better choice. Also, for small sellers, FBA is the only way that two-day shipping to buyers is affordable. Examine and compare FBM vs. FBA, considering costs such as wages, warehousing, storage fees, picking and packing fees, shipping fees and more. Also consider the higher cashflow typically garnered by FBA items, since sellers using FBA may be able to charge slightly more and most certainly get more Buy Box exposure.

Here is a real-life example. There is a fast-selling, expensive specialty toothpaste on Amazon.

- The FBA price is $24.95, which garners the Buy Box. Amazon charges the seller a $3.74 referral fee and $3.86 for pick, pack, and ship. This provides a net profit of $17.35 to the seller, excluding the cost of goods sold.
- The FBM price is $23.95, since the seller cannot command the FBA premium from buyers. Amazon charges the seller a $3.59 referral fee, and the seller spends approximately $4.50 for picking, packing, and shipping the order. This provides a net profit of $15.76 to the seller, excluding the cost of goods sold.

Customer experience. Do you feel the need to control the customer experience? With FBA, Amazon handles the entire fulfillment process, from picking and packing to returns and customer service messages. While this can be convenient, it also means that you have almost no oversight over how your products are packaged and presented to customers. With FBM, there is more control. You make or source the product, store the product, package it, and ship it. There's more flexibility in how it's presented and unboxed by the buyer. Additionally, you'll be able to respond to buyer inquiries and concerns directly, which can help build trust and loyalty with your customers. Of course, customer support services can be time-consuming and costly, with no guarantees that your customer's experience is any better or worse than FBA.

Flexibility. With FBM, you're working your approach, your plan, your way. You have the freedom to ship your items whenever and wherever, from your own warehouse or from a third-party logistics provider. You have more range to package and label products (Amazon guidelines still apply). There are more constraints with FBA. It means you ship your items to Amazon's fulfillment centers following their rules. It means you adhere to more of Amazon's strict guidelines for packaging and labeling individual products. It means potential foibles and delays. Essentially, it's all Amazon's way in Amazon's time.

Whether you're a new seller or one who's been in the race for years, it's a smart exercise to evaluate the most affordable, valuable fulfillment approach. For most sellers I know, a blended approach using both FBM and FBA works well.

It helps manage costs and keeps sellers from putting all their eggs in the Amazon FBA basket (which is riskier than you think).

Consider holding back approximately 10 percent to 20 percent of FBA inventory for merchant fulfillment. That way, if Amazon fails to stock your inventory in a timely manner, you can continue to sell and ship from your location. In addition, ship hazmat items from your own warehouse, rather than racking up Amazon's expensive fees for these types of products. Finally, if you have particularly large or heavy items for sale, consider shipping those yourself to avoid Amazon's dimensional fees.

What Kind of Seller Gets the Most Out of FBA?

Certain seller avatars scream out for FBA, while others may benefit from a mixed strategy or even FBM selling.

The Side Hustler, Brand Builder, and Lifestyle Impresario should embrace FBA, which frees up critical time and enables sellers to ship in inventory based on their own schedule. Orders come in and get fulfilled—no fuss, no muss.

Corporate Growth Hackers and Big Brand Product Launchers likely have internal fulfillment operations with affordable shipping costs. Should they choose FBA? Maybe— if they want to avoid additional fulfillment burdens in-house, and if they enjoy the Amazon handling of returns and customer service.

Classic Entrepreneurs will treat this like any other business decision—by the numbers. Most folks I know in this archetype do choose FBA.

The Basics of Shipping to FBA

There are stringent rules for shipping goods to FBA warehouses. Sellers cannot do it their way. They must do it Amazon's way. While many of the requirements seem like common sense, they are not simply suggestions. Straying afoul of Amazon's rules can result in:

- Customer complaints about bad product quality or wrong product received.
- Correction of shipments by Amazon FBA, which can make it take longer to receive inventory.
- Additional fees when Amazon decides that inventory was not prepared and shipped properly.
- Suspension of inbound shipping privileges.

Let's go over the basic steps of shipping into the FBA warehouse:

1. Create a shipping plan. In Seller Central, you designate how many units of each ASIN you wish to send. The app then creates a shipping plan, telling you where to send inventory. It walks you through the steps, from inventory prep to choosing a carrier.
2. Understand your inventory. Do your items need to be stored in a hazmat warehouse because they include hazardous materials? Does your inventory require special prep, such as polybagging or warning stickers? The Amazon Seller app will alert you to the possibilities, but you are still responsible for prepping correctly if Amazon doesn't make you aware of potential problems.

3. Prep your inventory. Don't skip steps. (More on this later.)

4. Pack your boxes carefully. The goal is zero movement, meaning that inventory isn't sloshing around inside the boxes. Place dunnage at the bottom, top, and around the sides of boxes for most items. Dunnage must not be newspaper, which can leave ink on products or workers' hands. Crumpled kraft paper, bubble wrap and similar materials work best. Boxes may not exceed fifty pounds, unless a single item being shipped to FBA is over that weight.

5. Use an Amazon partnered carrier to ship your inventory if possible. The discounts are substantial. Right now, that typically means sending units via UPS.

6. Require your carrier to scan the label of every single box when they receive it. This is your proof that they took possession in case shipments are lost. Alternatively, you may be able to create a manifest with a single barcode that can be scanned to receive all boxes, depending on the carrier.

7. Keep your shipping documentation until the shipment is received in-full at the Amazon warehouse—at a minimum.

More Annoying Details for Inbound Shipping to FBA

Prepping inbound FBA shipments can be more complicated than most sellers want to acknowledge. Again, most of the requirements seem like common sense. But a 3P seller's warehouse personnel may be tempted to just do it their own way, rather than understanding and strictly following Amazon's specific guidelines.

Inbound prep isn't just about putting items in boxes. It requires that your team ensures the correct items are being shipped in the correct condition. Create a process for inspecting inventory before it is shipped to Amazon:

- Match each ASIN to its listing detail page to ensure it's the correct product, with product packaging that matches the photos and description on the Amazon listing detail page.
- Ensure that the item is in brand-new condition, including a brand-new box without damage to corners, faded packaging, or other red flags that might make a buyer think the item is used or old.
- If the item is being listed as "used," ensure that you are using the correct condition based on Amazon's rules.

Package Like You Mean It

Don't assume Amazon Fulfillment Centers will take care of your inventory when picking and packing for buyers. Here are a few examples of things they do wrong:

- Glass candles shipped to customers in padded envelopes, causing them to shatter during transport.
- CDs shipped in padded envelopes and arriving with crushed cases.
- Delicate items like pressed powder makeup shipped in very large boxes with no dunnage.

Amazon FCs follow a standard called "prep guidance," which instructs their team members on how to pack items for shipping. There are a few problems with this:

- Sometimes, warehouse workers ignore prep guidance and pack the order in the way that is most convenient for them at the time.
- Sometimes, the FC runs out of the appropriate box size or envelope, so they use whatever is handy, even if it's far too large, too small, or doesn't provide the protection the product needs.
- Sometimes, the prep guidance is wrong in the Amazon system.

Sellers have to prep their inventory in such a way that it can survive inbound shipping to the FC, as well as shipment to the buyer. For example:

- If an item is fragile, it should be boxed with appropriate dunnage.
- Items that could leak if squeezed or dropped should be shrink-wrapped.
- Shrink-wrapping is ideal for anything that could accidentally open or spill, leading a customer to think it was used.
- Boxes must be the correct weight, so they are not crushed.
- Seals on boxes will prevent accidental opening.

The Seller with Two Left Shoes

The Amazon seller was baffled. His account had been shut down for selling inauthentic goods. But he sourced all inventory direct from the manufacturer. How could this be? He sold thousands of pairs of shoes every month. We discussed his business processes at length.

"Tell me about your boxes. Are they original branded shoeboxes?" I asked.

"Yes, of course," he said.

"And how are you keeping the boxes closed?" I asked.

Silence.

Turns out, the seller was not securing the shoeboxes. How did I know? Complaint after complaint said that pairs of shoes did not match. They were two different sizes, brands, or colors.

It's a perfect example of not thinking through how the FBA fulfillment center handles sellers' inventory. Unsecured boxes may spill out of cartons or open in the warehouse. It's unreasonable to expect that Amazon employees will carefully re-pair shoes that have become mixed up.

The solution? For this seller, I suggested plastic bands that could be used to secure the boxes without damaging the cardboard. Rubber bands will work for fast-moving items, but they should not be used if inventory will remain in the FC for long, because cold or heat could cause them to become brittle and break.

Selling Items as Sets

Many sellers send ASINs to the fulfillment center bundled together as a set. Unfortunately, workers at the Amazon warehouse can make tremendous mistakes by separating items that are meant to be sold together. For example, one client sold a two-pack of medicine that was shrink-wrapped together. Amazon workers broke the two-packs into singles, causing many complaints when buyers did not receive two items. Another client sold a bundle with multiple components in a polybag. Amazon workers broke the bundles up, which caused havoc.

How can sellers prevent these problems? Add a prominent sticker that says: "Sold as a set. Do not separate." This should stop the fulfillment center from making such egregious mistakes.

When in Doubt, Box, Polybag, or Shrink-Wrap

Amazon fulfillment centers are not sterile environments. Products are moved around multiple times. They become dusty and dirty. They are dropped on the floor. The best solution for most products? Keep them clean, safe, and in brand-new condition by placing them into protective packaging. This could mean placing them in a box, a polybag, or shrink-wrap.

This is an extra step that takes time and costs a few pennies. But it will more than pay off with fewer buyer complaints.

Amazon's Dirtiest FBA Secret: Used, Nasty, and Broken Returns

One reason buyers love Amazon is the friendly returns policy for FBA purchases. Amazon makes it easy for customers, who can look at their item and decide to send it back.

Unfortunately, buyers don't always return items in new condition. This might mean torn packaging, broken seals, or even used items.

Don't assume that Amazon's returns processing at the FBA warehouse is accurate—or even sanitary. Third-party sellers need to monitor returns and ensure that unacceptable items are not resold multiple times. Nutritional supplements with half the pills missing. Mouthwash with broken seals. Waffle makers with moldy batter clinging to them. These are only a few of the disgusting surprises that FBA sellers have experienced. Why? Because Amazon's FBA returns handling processes are, to put it kindly, lacking.

When an order is sent back to the FBA warehouse, Amazon personnel are supposed to inspect it carefully. They are charged with determining if the item is still in "new" condition. If so, it is placed into the seller's fulfillable inventory. If not, it is placed in unfulfillable. A third possible scenario involves Amazon repackaging the item. This happens when the product is in new condition, but the packaging is not. Amazon reserves the right to repackage it and place it back into fulfillable inventory. (The setting that once allowed sellers to turn off repackaging has been taken away. Sorry, folks, you're stuck with it.)

Amazon's warehouse employees are graded on the number of transactions they conduct per hour. Human nature dictates that this leads to inaccuracy as employees try to meet or beat the required work level. Quality naturally suffers, and items that should never be placed into fulfillable inventory are resold.

Another problem occurs when Amazon puts returns back into fulfillable inventory from categories that are supposed to be disposed of or not required to be mailed back to the warehouse. Supplements and food are a good example. These items should never be resold, but often are anyway.

The most worrisome scenarios with bad returns involve products that a 3P seller stocks over the long term. The higher volume you sell over time, the more potentially bad returns are sent back to the Amazon warehouse. There are a few strategies that 3P sellers can employ to combat the problem:

- For private-label products, add a printed seal. Include language such as "if seal is broken, item is not new." This seal is not for buyers. It's for personnel on Amazon's FBA returns processing teams. This way, they will be more likely to place an opened item into unfulfillable inventory.

- Sell down or sell through. For products you replenish, allow your stock to sell through. Alternatively, sell it down and then place a removal order for the remaining units. In the meantime, restock with a new batch under a different Fulfillment Network Stock Keeping Unit (FNSKU), which consists of an alphanumeric code and matching, unique barcode. This way, bad stock being resold multiple times will be removed from the FBA warehouse.

Just Say No to Commingling Amazon FBA Inventory

It's rare that I make a definitive, blanket statement about how to sell on Amazon. I'm a firm believer that there are many ways to skin the Amazon-selling cat. Plus, different sellers have varying levels of risk tolerance. But commingling allows me to break my "what's best for you" rule and declare that commingling is a bad choice for any and all FBA sellers.

When sellers create inbound FBA shipments, some ASINs offer two options: use the product's existing UPC or attach an FNSKU sticker. The product's existing UPC is the barcode that already exists on most manufactured products. If a seller chooses this option, their inventory is commingled. When a seller is prepping FBA inventory, they print an FNSKU sticker for each item, which is how Amazon links a specific unit of inventory to the exact seller who sent it to the warehouse.

When FBA inventory arrives at the Amazon FC, it can be handled in one of two ways:

- Commingled inventory is all put together in a bin, no matter who the seller of record might be. When an order for Seller A's unit of inventory arrives, it may be fulfilled by any of the commingled units Amazon has on hand—from any seller.
- Stickered inventory is segregated by seller. When an order for Seller A's unit of inventory arrives, it is supposed to be fulfilled specifically from Seller A's available stock. (More on the exceptions later.)

Why avoid commingling? You're a good seller. You work hard to ensure your inventory is authentic and in great shape. So why risk your orders being fulfilled with a bad seller's inventory? Here are real-world examples I've personally seen as the result of commingling:

- Counterfeit board games were sent to the FC, and my client's orders were fulfilled with fakes sent in by another seller. My client was shut down by Amazon for counterfeit goods and had great difficulty proving they were not selling illegal products.
- Off-brand fakes from another seller were sold in place of name-brand items. These off-brand fakes were products that plug in but did not have UL certification. At least two units caught on fire, resulting in a safety suspension for my client.
- Tubes of lotion that did not include safety seals were fulfilled from another seller's inventory. These lotions were not shrink-wrapped, polybagged, or otherwise prepped. They leaked everywhere, resulting in complaints for my client, who carefully shrink-wraps all her inventory.
- Shoes that were likely counterfeit (poor stitching) and sometimes had signs of wear were fulfilled in place of my client's legitimate inventory. This resulted in a suspension for inauthentic products.
- Chinese sellers flooded a clothing listing with fakes, whose decals peeled off easily. This resulted in ASIN suspensions for my client.

And that's just off the top of my head. There are hundreds of ways to get in deep, deep trouble, with customers and with Amazon, when you commingle inventory. In addition, sellers risk high return rates for poor-quality items.

Alas, even for sellers who sticker every item, there is "de facto commingling" at the Amazon warehouse. For example, let's imagine that Seller A has a unit of Kleenex in a California warehouse. Seller B has the same unit of Kleenex in a Texas warehouse. A customer who lives in Florida purchases the Kleenex from Seller A. Amazon may choose to ship the Texas Kleenex to the customer, and then put the California inventory on a truck to Texas to replace it.

This is just one of many reasons de facto commingling occurs. But make no mistake—your account is still much better off if you prevent as much commingling as possible by stickering your items.

Don't Let Amazon Sticker or Prep Your Inventory

"Hey, FBA seller! Yeah, you! Want to prep your inventory a lot faster? Want to avoid that pesky step of stickering your items? Let Amazon do it for you! For the low, low price of 20 cents per item, the FBA Label Service will create labels and stick them on all your inbound inventory."

For high-volume sellers, the siren song of the FBA Label Service sounds pretty good:

- You need fewer team members to prep inventory.
- If you ship inventory directly from your contract manufacturer or distributor to the FBA warehouse, you don't have to worry about paying them to sticker items—or the risk of them stickering inventory incorrectly.
- It's one less headache to manage on your end.

Unfortunately, there are pretty high risks associated with the FBA Label Service. Simply put, they are really bad at their job. And when they make mistakes, it can literally cost your account. The reason is simple: Stickering isn't as easy as it sounds. As any FBA seller knows, the FNSKU sticker only includes a portion of the product description and it's not always clear or easy to understand. If you aren't intimately familiar with the inventory you're stickering, it's super-easy to make a critical mistake.

We've seen all of the following occur with the FBA Label Service:

- UPCs not completely covered by the FNSKU, as required by Amazon's FCs.
- Stickers for variations of a product mixed up. The blue version was stickered with the pink version's FNSKU, and vice-versa. (This is really bad for gender reveal items and has resulted in a lot of super-angry parents who thought they were having a Robert, only to be later told they were having a Roberta, or vice-versa.)
- Completely wrong stickers placed on items, for ASINs that the seller doesn't even have in their inventory. Imagine selling a bottle of Vitamin C drops for children, and the buyer instead received a box of jumbo paperclips. True story.

Here is the ultimate problem: When the Amazon Label Service messes up, they do not take responsibility. The blame still falls directly on the seller. Some scenarios include:

- ASINs suspended for sending out wrong versions of products. Ultimately, a bin check showed that the items were stickered with the wrong variation by the FBA Label Service. But Amazon would not accept that as a Plan of Action and required the seller to admit fault.

- An account suspended for sending out a single bottle of a product, rather than the two-pack promised on the listing. This occurred when the FBA Label Service broke apart two-packs that had been shrink-wrapped together and labeled each bottle separately. Again, Amazon took no responsibility.
- Refusals to refund the fees for mis-stickering items in situations like those above. Amazon will almost never give sellers back their money.
- Refusals to perform bin checks in the warehouse. The FBA team often repels sellers' requests for bin checks when sellers suspect that their items were mislabeled by Amazon. This leaves sellers with two unattractive options: continue to try and sell-through inventory that may be mislabeled or pay to remove it for inspection.

What are the alternatives to Amazon's stickering and prep services?

1. Hire and train low-cost staff members to label your inventory. Ultimately, their accuracy will be superior to the FBA service, and they will likely cost less as well.
2. Work with your supplier to train their employees on proper stickering technique. Provide them with written documentation, as well as verbal instructions.
3. Have your contract manufacturer print your FNSKU directly on the product packaging, so no labeling is required.

Stale Sellers: Don't Let Expired Inventory Kill Your Account

Do you sell items with expiration dates via FBA? If so, I'll bet you are breaking the rules, and it's putting your ASINs—and maybe your account—in jeopardy.

Darlene loved to sell limited-edition potato chips with unusual flavors. But it was her third account suspension. Why? Potato chips have super-quick expiration dates. Same for the special-edition Oreos sold by Muhammed. He enjoyed the super-high ROI for these snacks, and he thought that Amazon FBA promised to sell his inventory first-in-first-out. But an expired package always seemed to make its way to the customer, who complained mightily when their soggy cookies didn't satisfy.

Most sellers don't pay close attention to the rules for expired products. But more importantly, they don't apply best practices that can ensure a good customer experience. Why should you care? When an Amazon seller sends expired inventory to customers, Amazon sees that as a behavior right up there with selling inauthentic goods. The item is no longer usable. It is trash. And customers deserve better.

First, let's review the rules for expired inventory. Here's what the folks at the FBA warehouse are going by:

- Inventory needs a readable expiration date if it is a topical or consumable product (including nutritional supplements) for human or animal consumption. And yes, it needs an expiry date even if there is not a date already on the packaging.
- If an item is in the Health and Beauty category, and it has a "period after opening" symbol, it should be

marked to expire nine hundred days after the date it is processed at the fulfillment center.

- Does it have a sell-by or best-by date? Amazon considers that the same as an expiration date.
- If you ship a food or beverage item to FBA, it must have a minimum remaining shelf life of more than 105 days. Items within fifty days of expiration date when they arrive at the warehouse will be marked for disposal.

Now for the parts that most sellers ignore:

- If a product has a consumption period because of regular use, add that period to the 105 days. For example, if you are selling a 120-day supply of vitamins, they need to have a shelf life of at least 225 days.
- Only one expiration date is allowed per ASIN per shipping box. Don't mix up expiration dates—it will confuse the warehouse and the process.
- If your item has an expiration date, the date must be printed in a font that is 36 points or larger. It should be printed in the format of MM-DD-YYYY or MM-YYYY. If the date is in a different format on the item's package, it needs to be covered up with the correct format, printed on a sticker.
- Case-packs, multi-packs, and display boxes must have the expiration date on the box or the bundle, as well as each individual item inside the box or bundle.
- Items that are polybagged or bubble wrapped require the expiry sticker on the outside of the package.

Why bother with expiry stickers? Amazon claims to treat inventory on a first-in-first-out basis. So in theory, your oldest items should sell first. In reality, this simply does not happen. In addition, too many sellers rely on Amazon to track their inventory expiration dates. Let's face it. The Amazon FBA warehouse has too much to do as it is. They are not going to track your expiration dates and reliably dispose of old inventory. For FBA inventory:

Follow the rules. Sticker every individual item with an expiry date. Amazon asks for large type because it is machine readable. This dramatically improves your chances that old, expired inventory will not be sold to a customer.

Track your expiration dates by inbound shipment. Create a unique SKU for different expiration dates to ensure that old SKUs are sold out before new SKUs are sent into the warehouse.

When your items are within fifty days of expiration, pull them from the warehouse immediately.

Don't expect customers to translate. If a product has a "period after opening" or lot number, do the research. Determine the appropriate date with the manufacturer, and label it accordingly with an expiration date.

Best practices are a little different for Merchant Fulfilled Network (MFN) sellers, who ship their own orders:

If it's hard to read, add a label. Many sellers in Health and Personal Care assume that MFN shipments don't need expiration dates. While this is technically true, it can lead to problems. Customers want to know the expiration date. If it's difficult to decipher, add a sticker with the correct date.

If it's from overseas, add a label. Products from other countries typically print expiry dates in DD-MM-YYYY format. This can lead to complaints of expired products—even when they are not. Add a sticker so that customers are not confused.

If it has a lot number or "period after opening" date, add a label. Again, reassure your customers. Tell them when the expiration date actually is, so they will not accuse you of selling old product.

Learn to Make Just-in-Time Inventory Work for You

I'm reading the tea leaves. All evidence points to Amazon embracing just-in-time (JIT) inventory principles for FBA sellers. The idea? Inventory doesn't sit in the warehouse for more than a few days. It arrives "just in time" to be shipped right back out to the buyer.

- For decades, JIT has reasonably been hailed as a cost-saving, efficient method for managing inventory. But a network of 3P sellers sending FBA inventory to fulfillment centers is more akin to a herd of cats than a manufacturing supply chain. As a result, Amazon is limiting quantities sellers can send to FBA, and their receiving operations are slow as molasses. Inventory runs out even if new stock is sitting in receiving for days or weeks. This results in stock-outs, lower bestseller ranks, lost sales, and frustration for third-party sellers.

Let's be real. JIT will be fraught with problems for sellers. I get it, Amazon. You are running out of warehouse space. You are trying to be efficient. You don't want dead inventory taking up valuable shelves and bins. But this will not go smoothly.

This is all a hassle. But Amazon ain't going back. They are expecting more from you. Play the game to win. Have an FBA offer and an MFN offer available at all times:

Sling your own boxes. This is your chance to gain a competitive advantage by merchant-fulfilling your products. The process is simpler than most FBA sellers assume it will be.

Find a fulfillment house. If it's not possible—or attractive—for you to pack and ship boxes, hire a fulfillment house. This is a great long-term strategy as well since there are times during holidays and crises when MFN listings can out-perform FBA.

When Things Go Wrong with an ASIN

Sometimes, Amazon suspends an ASIN or a seller account. This means that Amazon will not allow this item to be sold. There is an appeal process, but it can be time-consuming.

Amazon gives sellers a limited time to remove inventory from its FCs when accounts or ASINs are suspended. If the seller doesn't act fast enough, Amazon will destroy it.

When a suspension occurs, inventory at the Amazon warehouse goes on a timer. Amazon designates these units at the FC as "unfulfillable." They remain in unfulfillable status until one of these things happens:

1. The seller wins their appeal, pushing the inventory into fulfillable status.
2. The seller places a removal order for their inventory, choosing to recall or destroy it.
3. Amazon "destroys" the inventory.

Inventory Hits "At Risk" Status

When inventory reaches sixty days of "unfulfillable" status, Amazon can destroy it. The reasons for this are obvious. Amazon cannot be a warehouse for millions of units of inventory that are no longer eligible for sale. This is frustrating for sellers in the throes of the appeals process. In the midst of the back-and-forth with Seller Performance, nothing ratchets up the stress like a threat to throw away your stuff.

It's a bit of a mystery how and why Amazon sets its sixty-day timer. In reality, the time from suspension to inventory destruction seems much closer to ninety or 120 days. Regardless, the deadline that sellers should focus on is the one supplied in the warning email from Amazon. Amazon sends the warning email thirty days before destroying inventory. A reminder comes five days prior to inventory destruction. But there's a caveat. Amazon is completely unreliable when it comes to the thirty-day warning. Amazon shocks more than a few sellers by destroying their inventory at the twenty-eight-day mark, or sooner. It's difficult to receive compensation for this error.

The safest course of action is to remove inventory well ahead of the deadline. Sellers object to this. It's expensive to remove inventory, especially in large quantities. Plus, Amazon FBA does not treat removal orders with care. Rather, they see removal order inventory as "garbage," and they pack it accordingly.

The best advice? Appeal immediately. If your account or ASIN is taken down, do not hesitate. Give yourself the best chance of winning reinstatement before Amazon sends the dreaded destruction notice.

The Dark Side of FBA

FBA opens endless opportunities for sellers. But as with any exciting opportunity, there are potential downfalls. In the case of FBA, mistakes by Amazon's FCs can eat up a seller's bottom line. In fact, we estimate that an average seller sees negative impacts to between 5 percent and 10 percent of their inventory at the hands of FBA.

Amazon does make sellers whole for a tiny sliver of these FBA errors. These "automatic" reimbursements lull some into a sense of security and a belief that Amazon has their back. That attitude, however, can be costly. Fortunately, with diligence and hard work, sellers can minimize these unjust costs and ensure Amazon pays back every penny it owes.

Profit-killer #1: Inventory from inbound FBA shipments is not received. This is far and away the most significant profit-killer for Amazon FBA sellers. A business sends hundreds or thousands of units to Amazon FCs. Amazon then reports that some or all of the inventory never arrived. Most sellers rely on Amazon Partnered Carriers to ship inventory to the Amazon FCs. They create shipments via Seller Central, and their inbound shipments are then handed off to UPS or a carrier that can handle pallets and truckloads. These carriers provide a tracking number, proving that the seller gave them the inbound shipment. The shipments arrive at Amazon FCs, where they are signed for at the dock. Amazon warehouse workers receive the items. These individuals scan either case packs or individual units of inventory, depending upon the shipment type. Ideally, the number of units scanned matches the shipment's original contents perfectly. Alas, a significant portion of shipments come up short at the Amazon warehouse. Amazon declares that the seller didn't send all the units. And suddenly, that shipment of three hundred sellable items is only 265 sellable items. Amazon expects the seller to eat the remaining thirty-five units— even though they are somewhere in the FC. In some cases, unreceived inventory can add up to just a few dollars. But there are circumstances where these errors can cost a large seller hundreds of thousands of dollars. Over time, it really adds up. So, what's a seller to do? Once a shipment is received and listed as "closed" by Amazon, if not all items in the shipment were received, the seller can open a case via Seller Central. Amazon then investigates the case and decides what to do next. This might be reimbursement to the seller after documentation is provided by the seller, reimbursement (but not enough) to the seller (more on this later), or a denial of reimbursement. If Amazon denies reimbursement, sellers can reopen the case, provide additional documentation, and ask for reconsideration. Pro tip: Maintain a database of invoices and shipping documents for all shipments to Amazon FCs. Share these with your reimbursements team—whether internal or external—so they have needed details at their fingertips.

Profit-killer #2: Amazon unfairly denies claims for reimbursement. "Investigation complete." Those are two of the most frustrating words that pop up in a Seller Central account. When Amazon doesn't properly receive inventory, or loses, damages, or otherwise mishandles inventory, sellers can ask for an investigation. The words "investigation complete" can be Amazon's dismissive way of saying, "We're right, and you're wrong." Many times, however, the mistakes were clearly made at the Amazon FC. For example, Amazon will show that it accepted boxes at the dock. But then, it will claim the boxes were all empty—despite bills of lading that clearly state each box weighed twenty to fifty pounds. Sometimes, Amazon eventually corrects the mistake. But what happens when Amazon FBA simply refuses to reimburse the seller for lost items? That's where robust appeals come into play. Sellers must fight back to get reimbursed. This usually starts with a case sent via Seller Central, asking the FBA team to investigate. If that fails, another step is to request a phone call from the Captive team. This is a high-level Seller Support team at Amazon, which can chase down the issue. If Amazon still refuses to acknowledge their mistake, it's time for executive escalations. These are succinct, fact-filled emails sent to key teams or executives inside of Amazon. Pro tip: Choose a reimbursements service with robust appeal capabilities. They can help escalate high-value reimbursements claims to the right Amazon teams and increase your chances of winning.

Profit-killer #3: Amazon loses and damages inventory. Lost and damaged inventory can happen in countless ways. It's not an exaggeration to say that a dropped bottle can roll under a shelf at the FC and remain there for months or years. Items are also misfiled, placed in the wrong bin, or put on the wrong truck for transshipment between warehouses. (I once had an item that I had not sold in two years pop up in my available inventory. It was "found" in the FBA warehouse.) When it comes to "finding" items and filing claims for lost and damaged inventory, Amazon definitely has an advantage over sellers. There are several reports in Seller Central that must be parsed, compared, and analyzed to determine which inventory items are truly missing. It's not a task for the impatient, nor for the time-pressed. There is also risk involved. If reports are not understood and properly interpreted, not all claims will be filed. Worse, a lack of understanding can lead to inaccurate claims by a seller, which can result in sanctions by Amazon or even the loss of selling privileges. It behooves sellers to employ a reliable reimbursements service to ensure they uncover every inventory shortage that occurs in their account over time. Pro tip: Keep an eye on the calendar. These types of reimbursements are available for eighteen months, and not one day more.

Profit-killer #4: Amazon reimburses the seller for inventory claims—but not enough. When Amazon accepts a claim for reimbursement, they are supposed to credit the seller fairly. This doesn't always happen. First, let's talk about what constitutes "fair." A reasonable reimbursement is the cash amount Amazon would transfer to the seller, less fees, if the item had been sold. In other words, the seller receives exactly what they would have gotten if an Amazon customer bought the item and Amazon fulfilled it. (Amazon also has the option to reimburse the seller by providing them with a replacement inventory item.) Sometimes, however, the reimbursement amount is far less than fair. In these instances, the seller must open a case and ask for more. For example, a seller shipped in a box of new private-label products as a test run. Amazon lost the shipment and reimbursed the seller at a rate under the cost of goods. It required multiple back-and-forth emails with Seller Support, as well as submission of invoices, to get a fair reimbursement. Pro tip: Provide clear evidence that Amazon shorted you. That can include your own recent sales history, invoices, and more. If you can't provide data, don't waste time appealing.

Profit-killer #5: Amazon messes up customer returns. Amazon set the Gold Standard for generous customer returns policies. Sometimes, however, the e-commerce giant's generosity to customers can end up harming sellers.

Here are a few ways that customer returns can come back to bite sellers right in the inventory:

- The customer returns the item, but Amazon doesn't add it back to inventory or reimburse the seller.
- The customer receives a refund, but they never return the item.
- Amazon grants the customer a refund that is more than they were originally charged.
- The customer sends back a wrong item or item with missing components, and Amazon accepts it.
- Amazon allows the customer to return an item outside of the return policy. (Sometimes, Amazon customer service goes crazy and allows returns even two years after purchase!)

Sellers can file claims for all these errors. It's especially important to file claims in February and March, when Amazon sees the greatest customer abuse in terms of bad returns, out-of-policy exceptions, and more. Pro tip: If you remove inventory from the Amazon FCs, inspect it carefully to see if Amazon committed the above mistakes and owes you money as a result.

Profit-killer #6: Amazon mismeasures an item and charges excess fees. Many of the fees that Amazon sellers pay to FBA are based on the weight and dimensions of their products. This stands to reason; larger items take up more space in Amazon warehouses, resulting in higher storage fees and transshipping costs. Heavier and larger items require more expensive packaging and shipping costs. Amazon relies on a machine called a Cubiscan to determine the size and weight of products. Unfortunately, this technology is not always accurate. The machines may be dirty. The machines may not have been calibrated and maintained properly at the FBA warehouse. Or there may be user error involved. Whatever the reason, bad Cubiscan data has cost Amazon sellers millions of dollars. It's important to conduct an ASIN-by-ASIN audit of what Amazon shows as the weight and dimensions of inventory items. If the numbers are more than 20 percent off, or if they push an item into a more expensive size category, sellers should request remeasurement via a case in Seller Central. If the numbers come back as inaccurate, the seller must be prepared to reply with photographic evidence of the real measurements. For example, a client's product was repeatedly mismeasured by Amazon FBA. After our appeals, they were reimbursed more than $18,000 for elevated fees on that single ASIN over nine months. Pro tip: If you discover Amazon has been overcharging based on product dimensions, you can request a refund of those fees going back eighteen months. Don't expect a full refund, but fight for what you can get. Appeals companies can help with this as well.

Profit-killer #7: Amazon charges fees for the wrong category. Some categories are more expensive than others. Amazon's referral fee for most categories is 15 percent. There are notable exceptions such as video game consoles, clothing, and gift cards, which cost more. If an ASIN belongs in home and garden, but is put into clothing and accessories, the 2 percent difference in fees really adds up over time. For one large seller we know, this very mistake added up to a quarter-million dollars in inaccurate fees over two years. Pro tip: Past overcharges for category can be appealed, just like overcharges for weight and dimensions. Be prepared to provide detailed information about your losses, and don't expect a full and fair refund.

Profit-killer #8: Amazon destroys a seller's inventory without permission. In rare—but very expensive—circumstances, Amazon destroys a seller's inventory. This can happen as a one-off situation. Or it can be a tremendous mistake in concert with enforcement by Seller Performance, as mentioned above. Appealing this horrible error often requires escalation to an executive team. Pro tip: This inventory is not usually "destroyed." It shows up in the Amazon Warehouse Deals seller account, or it is liquidated out of the FCs. Of course, Amazon keeps the proceeds in either case.

Profit-killer #9: Amazon grants a reimbursement, but never gives the seller the cash. Welcome to the accounting torture chamber, where a seller must compare every promised reimbursement to their actual financials on Seller Central to find the errors. Pro tip: This is one more reason to use a reimbursements service. You have better things to do with your time, but you still need that money back!

Profit-killer #10: Amazon fails to fulfill a removal order. This is a rarity, but easily missed by most sellers. Why? Because the folks taking care of Seller Central and the team managing the seller's warehouse are usually two totally different groups of people. When removal orders are placed, it can take Amazon FBA weeks or months to actually send the inventory back to the seller. This also creates a situation where the pending removal order falls down a memory hole. Making it worse, Amazon doesn't have a true deadline internally for these things. Pro tip: Keep a log of removal orders that is regularly handed off to whomever manages your warehouse. Check off orders as they are received, and file claims for any that are incomplete or damaged.

Chapter 7 Summary

- Amazon's FBA program offers the opportunity for 3P sellers to leverage the e-commerce leader's fulfillment, warehousing, and customer service capabilities.
- Most sellers benefit from using FBA, with backup options for FBM orders if inventory becomes unavailable via FBA.
- Sellers must keep a close eye on the costs associated with FBA, including regular reviews of the fees being paid for warehousing, referrals, and pick-and-pack.
- It's critical to continually audit the inventory being stored at FBA FCs to ensure Amazon reimburses sellers for lost, damaged, and otherwise mishandled goods.

What about you?

1. Have you created written instructions for your team, so they create inbound FBA shipments that comply with all applicable rules?

2. Consider hiring a reimbursements service to ensure that you are compensated for lost, missing and damaged FBA inventory, among other inflated fees.

3. How can your company have a backup FBM strategy to ensure that your listings are always live? Can you ship a limited number of orders with your existing infrastructure? Or should you hire a 3PL?

Part 3
Get Your Amazon Business off the Ground

CHAPTER 8

Buyer Experience Wins

No matter your seller avatar, one thing is for sure. If you sell on Amazon, you are expected to treat buyers exceptionally well. The question is, how can you accomplish this with every interaction? It is possible, with a little organization and a lot of understanding.

Earth's most customer-centric company. That's the goal of Amazon.com, where the customer comes first, last, and always. Amazon sets a high bar. The customer gets the benefit of the doubt, almost every time. That translates into problems for sellers:

- Acceptance of late returns, past the thirty-day window clearly stated in the rules for both buyers and sellers (with the exception of an even longer return window during the holiday season).
- A blind eye turned to used items, opened items, and even old, nasty items that are returned for an exchange or refund.
- Refunds, concessions, and gift cards for even the smallest misstep, or no misstep at all.

While they can be frustrating for third-party sellers, Amazon's customer-focused policies have created a loyal customer base hundreds of millions strong willing to pay subscription fees for Prime delivery and shell out a premium for items that are delivered quickly. They are also more likely to buy first from Amazon third-party sellers, rather than from other websites or brick-and-mortar stores.

At Amazon, third-party sellers can be replaced. So can vendors. But buyers? Buyers are indispensable. They carry massive lifetime value—especially loyal Prime members. When Amazon refers to being "buyer-centric," this is about more than just customer service. Amazon also cares about buyers' needs, preferences, and satisfaction.

This is important for sellers to know and understand. When buyers purchase items on Amazon.com, they often have no idea whether they bought directly from Amazon's retail operation (1P) or from a 3P seller. Amazon expects the world's best buyer experience to apply to all transactions— no matter who is the seller of record. That means that every third-party seller must develop a customer focus, buyer experience, and customer-facing attitude that meets or exceeds Amazon's expectations. Keep in mind that Amazon buyers have grown accustomed to being put first, in every transaction. They assume that they will be treated similarly by every third-party seller.

What a Buyer-Focused Company Looks Like

If 3P sellers wish to be successful on the Amazon platform, it's not enough to simply acknowledge the values put forth by Amazon corporate. A wholehearted embrace of these principles maximizes the chances of winning over the long term:

Customer obsession. Amazon is dedicated to understanding and meeting the evolving needs and expectations of its customers. The company strives to provide a seamless and convenient shopping experience by offering a wide selection of products, competitive pricing, and fast and reliable delivery.

Customer reviews and ratings. Amazon actively encourages customers to provide feedback and reviews on their purchases. Customer reviews play a significant role in helping other shoppers make informed buying decisions. Amazon uses this feedback to improve product selection, quality, and overall customer experience.

Personalization and recommendations. Amazon leverages algorithms and data analytics to personalize the shopping experience for individual customers. The company recommends products based on a customer's browsing and purchasing history, increasing the likelihood of finding relevant and appealing items.

Easy returns and refunds. Amazon has established a streamlined and customer-friendly return and refund policy. This policy allows customers to return products easily and receive refunds or replacements quickly, enhancing customer satisfaction and trust.

Customer service. Amazon places great importance on providing responsive and helpful customer service. The company offers various support channels and aims to address customer inquiries and concerns promptly and effectively.

Continuous innovation. Amazon is committed to continuously improving its services and offerings to better serve its customers. The company invests heavily in research and development, exploring new technologies and features to enhance the customer experience.

Long-term relationships. Amazon seeks to build long-term relationships with its customers rather than focusing solely on individual transactions. By prioritizing customer satisfaction and loyalty, Amazon aims to foster lasting customer relationships and repeat business.

By embracing a buyer-centric approach, Amazon strives to create a customer experience that exceeds expectations, fosters trust, and encourages repeat business. This customer-centric focus has been instrumental in Amazon's growth and success as one of the world's largest online marketplaces.

Why Sellers Need to Be Buyer-Centric

Longtime Amazon sellers know that one key to winning online is to provide excellent customer service. Amazon prides itself on the buyer experience and ensuring timely, solution-driven help. It expects the same standards and customer service operations from its sellers.

After all, former Amazon CEO Jeff Bezos once had this to say: "The most important single thing is to focus obsessively on the customer. Our goal is to be earth's most customer-centric company."

Amazon's internal philosophy is to keep its eye on the customer, not the competition, to grow and sustain its business. Good customer service centers around meticulously listening to and resolving your customers' needs and desires. If you do not constantly seek opportunities to improve your customer service, your relationships stagnate. For a seller, that relationship means repeat buyers. To be a successful Amazon seller, the relationship—and the repeat buyers—are paramount. And when polled, buyers cite customer service among the reasons they re-patronize a seller. It's not all about flashy product photography or prices. In fact, no matter how unique your product is or how talented your team is, customers will remember the direct interaction they have with your company. If it's a bad interaction, they'll tell others and won't shop with you again.

I frequently have Amazon sellers ask me how they can improve their customer service. The answer to this question varies, but here are a few universal truths that help sellers set themselves apart from the competition:

- Are you efficient? Efficiency doesn't just mean getting a task done as fast as possible; it means answering customer service inquiries in a timely, organized fashion. This lets you address truly complex buyer concerns with more time on your side. If you're buried under customer queries and questions, and have no time, personnel, or process to quickly respond, you're in trouble.

- Do you have great templates? Creating templates for common questions, generating autoresponders for quick responses, and using other time-saving tools will alleviate the burdens and backflows of customer interaction, and prevent customers from being disappointed—and disappearing. It also will remove emotion from the situation in case you are frustrated by the customer's queries. Pre-written templates help you sound the same, every time, to every customer. They also enable you to push work down to other team members or virtual assistants, with excellent end results.

- Is your tone appropriate? Responding to buyers with empathy, patience, and consistency defuses tension before it can build. Most buyers want their concerns to be seen and acknowledged. As difficult as it can be, kind words bring rewards.

- Are you being clear? We all think we're superb communicators. Most of us are not. Review your communications. Are you being clear, concise, and accurate? How's your tone? Do you appear courteous or curt? Some customers will be angry, and others, full of questions. And some will be chatty. The trick is knowing how to handle all these customers and provide the same service every time. But above all, write with clarity and solution-finding in mind. Avoid hostility, sarcasm, and criticism. Check to make sure you are not unclear or ambiguous. Don't kill the chance of repeat sales for a quick stab at the customer.

- Create solutions, not barriers. When you're a buyer, you want the retailer or department store to solve your problem, be it a refund, exchange, or just empathizing with your experience. Amazon buyers want the same thing. Be sure to have clear, concise policies about returns. Be mindful that you might need to bend occasionally to satisfy a buyer.

Poor customer service can leave a lasting stain on public perception. It is dangerous for a seller to not satisfy the customer, or to become snarky or critical. In ten seconds, an angry buyer can make vicious claims against you on social media. One tweet or Facebook post can wipe out a seller in seconds. It's not worth it.

Be honest with yourself. Look critically at all phases of your customer service operations. If you're not consistently achieving all five of the above points, go back to the drawing board. Getting this right sooner is always better and will help you scale your business to greater heights. Also, share with your team that customer service on Amazon is the cornerstone for ultimate success or failure; that each customer interaction will be measured on a scale from terrible to terrific. Shoot for terrific! It encourages repeat business and strengthens customer loyalty.

Which brings us back to the question, "What is good customer service?" It is customer-focused attention with empathy and active listening. Bring these to your organization and you'll be successful on Amazon over time.

Buyer Experience Goes Far beyond Messages

Most sellers think that how they answer buyer-seller messages on Amazon makes up the entirety of the buyer experience. Wrong. There's much more to it. Amazon customers expect:

High-quality products. Offer products that meet or exceed customer expectations in terms of quality, functionality, and durability. Conduct thorough quality-control checks to ensure the products are in optimal condition before shipping them to customers, including external packaging.

Accurate product descriptions. Provide detailed and accurate product descriptions, including specifications, features, and any limitations. Use high-quality product images from various angles to showcase the product effectively. Transparency and honesty in product information build trust with customers.

Competitive pricing. Price your products competitively to attract customers. Consider factors such as manufacturing or sourcing costs, fees, and market demand. Conduct regular pricing analysis to ensure your prices remain competitive while still maintaining profitability.

Fast and reliable shipping. Fulfill orders promptly and communicate shipping updates to customers. Use Amazon's FBA service for fast and reliable shipping. If using other fulfillment methods, ensure efficient order processing and timely shipment.

Clear return and refund policy. Establish a clear and customer-friendly return and refund policy. Make it easy for customers to initiate returns or refunds if they are dissatisfied with the product. Promptly process returns and provide excellent customer service throughout the process.

Encourage customer feedback. Respond to customer reviews, both positive and negative, to show your dedication to customer satisfaction.

Continuous improvement. Regularly evaluate and improve your seller performance based on customer feedback and data. Monitor customer reviews, ratings, and satisfaction metrics. Use feedback as a valuable source of insight to enhance product quality, customer service, and overall buyer experience.

By focusing on these strategies, you can create a positive and memorable buyer experience on Amazon. Satisfied customers are more likely to become repeat buyers, leave positive reviews, and recommend your products to others, ultimately contributing to the long-term success of your Amazon business.

The Reality for Third-Party Sellers

If a seller doesn't live up to those standards, what happens? Warnings, suspensions, and other costly enforcement actions can be the result of:

- A-to-Z claims against merchant-fulfilled sellers
- Negative feedback that is ever harder to remove

- Negative product reviews for private-label sellers
- Fewer repeat sales to happy customers

As every good seller knows, A-to-Z claims plus negative feedback creates a high Order Defect Rate. And this can create an account suspension. Don't put black marks on your Amazon account by mistreating customers. Follow Amazon's lead to provide amazing customer service. This will reduce your risk—and your blood pressure.

Keep items in stock. This especially applies for brands. In-stock rate is critical to Amazon success and can affect both Buy Box availability and storage space at FBA.

Answer customer messages quickly. Shoot for an average response time under eight hours. Amazon answers even faster, so a long wait makes customers antsy.

Apologize when needed. Don't hesitate to take responsibility when the customer is unhappy—even if it wasn't completely your fault.

Pay for quality shipping—especially overseas. Not all package delivery was created equal. Ensure that you choose reliable, high-quality carriers. Cheaper is not always better.

Look for trends. Even when your customers don't reach out to you directly, they are leaving clues about your business. High returns show dissatisfaction with specific ASINs. Bad feedback or negative reviews reveal problems with orders or products. Run reports weekly and uncover the biggest problem areas. Solve two problems a week, and soon your business will be more profitable than ever.

Hit the refund button—fast. Don't make customers beg for refunds. If they are unhappy, just give the money back, if possible. This will head off all manner of complaints and customer service problems. Set a price point cutoff. If the price of the item is below X, your customer service team is empowered to immediately provide a refund.

Never, ever argue. Customers can be frustrating. And let's face it—not everybody is honest. Some are trying to get something for nothing. That simply doesn't matter to Amazon. Treat every customer as a valuable, important person, no matter what.

Product Quality and Voice of the Customer

Sellers must understand how well their Amazon presence is—or isn't—being managed. This is especially true for brands and applies whether the brand maintains its own seller account or relies on a few handpicked third-party sellers to move its product on Amazon.

First and foremost, the brand must maintain high product quality for buyers. The team members managing the seller account must stay on top of key reports and data. One of the most valuable of these is the Voice of the Customer section of Seller Central, which can quickly reveal problems with products. For example, by reviewing our clients' Voice of the Customer data, my team has uncovered:

- A dish soap that angered many customers because of sticky leakage
- A national clothing brand with a single line of shirts that ran too small
- A replacement car part that was being wrongly fulfilled with a generic, rather than a branded, item

The examples are endless. That's why sellers require continual monitoring and review of their data. And here's the secret. The seller must remedy these problems—before Amazon "fixes" them by suspending the product or the seller. Amazon expects more than the Golden Rule from sellers. Buyers must be given every benefit of the doubt. Easy returns. Perfect product quality. Fast email responses. And products they can count on.

Chapter 8 Summary

- Amazon considers itself the most customer-centric company in the world. It expects third-party sellers to take the same attitude across all phases of their businesses.
- Being buyer focused goes far beyond the way customer service messages are answered. It includes things like product quality, pricing, in-stock rates, and more. Without happy customers, buyers cannot expect to enjoy high Buy Box percentages or repeat business.

- Voice of the Customer is a great tool inside Seller Central, which can surface problems with products early.

What about you?

1. If you do not have customer service messaging templates, create new ones today! Review the last ninety days of customer service queries to find the most common questions asked by buyers. Ensure that you create answers that are accurate and friendly in tone for all messages.

2. Train your team to use your updated templates, or find a service to handle your customer buyer-seller messaging.

3. Schedule time each week to review Voice of the Customer in Seller Central. Learn how it works and how to navigate the data. Once you've become familiar with the interface, train a virtual assistant or team member to review this section of Seller Central and provide you with an overview once a week.

CHAPTER 9

Keep Your Products Active and Selling

You've got a killer business plan. You know your goals, for the short term and the future. You've picked products and a fulfillment method.

That could all come to a screeching halt, if you run into problems with Amazon's internal "police." Large teams of Amazonians spend their time making sure that buyers are treated fairly, and that products are what they promise to be. This chapter will help you understand potential pitfalls, so you can ensure your business stays out of the Amazon doghouse.

Why Amazon Enforces against Sellers

For Amazon, account and ASIN suspensions are just part of doing business. Like any large company, Amazon has an extensive risk management strategy. This includes multiple departments and thousands of employees whose job is to ensure buyer safety on the Amazon platform; protect the company, its reputation, and its finances; and prevent criminal activity such as money laundering and sale of stolen or counterfeit goods.

When Amazon closes a seller account, the action can take many forms:

Account suspension or account deactivation. The seller can write an account appeal and ask for reinstatement. Amazon intends to read the appeals and consider reactivating the account.

Account block. This can happen immediately when Amazon detects seller behavior it considers to be egregious. A block can also occur after Amazon reviews a seller's appeals and rejects them. Amazon says it will not entertain additional appeals at this point in the process. (That is not necessarily true; reinstatement can be achieved for many accounts that have reached block status.)

Fraud block. If Amazon detects fraudulent activity in a seller account, it can block the seller's ability to log into Seller Central. This ultimately shuts down the account as well—permanently. Amazon does not accept appeals through regular channels after a fraud block. (Reinstatement in these circumstances requires communication to executive teams and individuals at Amazon.)

Types of Account Suspensions

There are more than a dozen common account suspensions that affect Amazon sellers. The most common include:

Counterfeit or inauthentic products. These suspensions are usually initiated after buyers complain about the products they receive. These complaints might claim that the items are fake, counterfeit, or poor quality. Inauthentic suspensions can also be the result of a wrong item sent out to customers.

Condition or used sold as new. These account deactivations also result from buyer complaints. In these cases, buyers have said they received damaged, opened, used or dirty products. Additional claims might be for broken seals, missing parts, and other indications an item was sold before and returned or sold before and used.

Expired products. Also based on buyer complaints, these suspensions occur when items are past their expiration or best by date. In addition, buyers might complain if they misunderstand, cannot read, or cannot find the expiration date on the product.

Late shipment rate. Amazon expects items to be shipped promptly by sellers who fill their own orders. If the number of late shipments rises above 4 percent, the account or the seller's merchant-fulfilled shipping privileges may be suspended.

Valid tracking rate. When a merchant fulfills an order, they must provide tracking information on Seller Central the same business day. When tracking details are entered late or incorrectly, or when fake tracking information is entered, Amazon may suspend the account or the seller's ability to ship their own orders.

Order defect rate. The order defect rate (ODR) may not rise above 1 percent, or Amazon may suspend the account. ODR is made up of negative seller feedback, A-to-Z claims, and chargebacks.

Pre-fulfillment cancel rate. Sellers are expected to fulfill the orders made on Amazon.com. If a seller cancels orders, there can be dire consequences. The pre-fulfillment cancel rate (PFCR) must remain below 2.5 percent.

Intellectual property complaints. Amazon allows brand owners to file intellectual property (IP) complaints against sellers for copyright infringement, trademark infringement and patent infringement. Depending upon the number and severity of complaints, this can lead to account deactivation.

Forged and manipulated documents. Amazon sometimes asks sellers for documents such as invoices, letters of authorization, product testing and shipment confirmations. If Amazon detects that these documents were forged or edited in any way, the account will be suspended.

Platform manipulation and fake reviews. Fake reviews, paid reviews, and incentivized reviews are not allowed on Amazon. In addition, Amazon will suspend seller accounts for fake reviews on competitor's products, upvoting and downvoting reviews, and similar behavior it sees as manipulative.

Best Seller Rank (BSR) manipulation. Sellers use a wide range of strategies to try and increase their BSR inorganically. Amazon bans many of these behaviors such as super URLs, chatbots, and more.

Listing abuse and variation abuse. This relatively rare suspension type occurs when sellers create duplicate listings, make storefront-specific offers, or guarantees on a listing, and create variations that break policy, among other violations.

Account verification. This occurs when Amazon decides a seller needs to provide documents verifying their identity—typically a passport or driver's license, as well as a utility bill showing they are a real person. Occasionally, more extensive documentation is needed.

Linked accounts. If Amazon detects that a seller is linked to an account that has been suspended or blocked from the platform, it can result in the suspension of their current account. Also, while sellers are allowed to have more than one selling account for a legitimate business reason, they may not sell the same ASINs on more than one account. Amazon considers a legitimate business reason to be something like selling products from two different categories on two different seller accounts, or selling private-label products on one account and wholesale items on another account.

Restricted products. Amazon can close an account that repeatedly offers products not allowed on the Amazon platform. This includes supplements with prohibited ingredients, certain weapons, drug paraphernalia and many more examples.

Retail drop-shipping. Sellers are not allowed to retail dropship on Amazon. This is where an order is placed, and the seller fulfills the order by purchasing it and having it shipped directly from another retailer such as Home Depot, Target, or even Amazon.com.

Code of conduct. These suspensions, also known as Violations of Section 3, are among the most challenging on Amazon. They occur when Amazon detects particularly bad behavior, such as intentionally circumventing Amazon's rules, harming other sellers, or hurting buyers.

Fraud. When Amazon detects fraudulent activity, it locks down a seller account immediately. This can occur when a bad guy gets access to an account and tries to steal the funds or inventory. It can also be the result of fraudulent sales, gift card fraud, money laundering, and other criminal activity.

The New Reality at Amazon—Appeal Every Suspended ASIN

In addition to suspending entire accounts, Amazon can suspend individual products. Suspended ASINs can be the bane of an Amazon seller's existence. Inventory stops moving. Cash stops flowing. And appealing the defect to Seller Performance can be time-consuming and difficult.

In the past, I recommended that sellers not appeal every ASIN defect, depending on the particular circumstances around each case. But recent changes to Amazon's enforcement regime have flipped that prior advice on its head. Now, I urge sellers to appeal every single ASIN defect they possibly can.

In fall 2022, Amazon rolled out a new method for policing seller accounts. In an effort to be more transparent with sellers, the company launched something called the Account Health Rating (AHR). Each seller account has an AHR score, which can range from 0 to 1,000. The stated purpose of the score is to let sellers know if their selling account is at risk of deactivation. There are three status levels:

1. A score of 200 to 1,000 is considered "Healthy." It is not at risk of deactivation.
2. A score of 100 to 199 is considered "At Risk." This means that Seller Performance believes the account is at risk of deactivation.
3. A score of 99 or lower is considered "Unhealthy." The account is either suspended or eligible for suspension at any time.

Keep in mind, even a perfect AHR score doesn't protect a seller account from deactivation. Seller Performance can immediately suspend accounts suspected of nefarious activities such as fraud or other actions that harm buyers, other sellers, or Amazon itself.

What makes an AHR score rise and fall? While the formula and exact number is hard to discern—much like Amazon's other black-box algorithms—the causes are clear. When a seller has not been warned for policy violations, and they also do not have any ASINs with defects, their score will rise as sales volume increases. They will easily stay above the 200 mark.

The score begins to fall when policy violations and ASIN-level defects are received. These include ASINs suspended or questioned regarding:

- Authenticity
- Suspected intellectual property violations
- Received intellectual property violations
- Product condition complaints, sometimes known as "used sold as new"
- Restricted products issues
- Safety complaints
- And more

Each defect is labeled by Amazon on a scale from "high impact" to "no impact." Unfortunately, that impact rating does not always clearly correlate with the change of the AHR score. Even defects labeled as "no impact" have pushed some accounts' AHR scores below the threshold of 200.

The Shock of a Sudden AHR Collapse

To understand why I now recommend appealing all ASIN defects, it helps to see a few examples of how the new AHR score can dramatically change.

For instance, one seller had a healthy AHR score in the 300 range. Overnight, they received multiple IP complaints from a single brand covering about a dozen ASINs. This immediately pushed the seller's AHR under the 200 threshold, resulting in an account suspension. Another seller had a catalog with about 1,200 products. Despite a nice volume of sales, just two "critical" defects for inauthentic pushed their AHR score from the 600s to a sub-200 number, and they were threatened with immediate suspension. A third seller had dozens of safety complaints they left unaddressed over time. Their AHR score was, nonetheless, in the healthy range. Then a slew of suspected IP violations over the course of a week destroyed their AHR score and resulted in account deactivation.

What is the lesson? Secrecy around the calculation of the AHR score, coupled with the uncertainty of selling on Amazon, makes any new defect a possible account killer. Sellers simply cannot stand by and watch their scores sink over time. Eventually, a defect or policy violation will put the account into "At Risk" or "Unhealthy" territory.

The remedy is to appeal every possible suspended ASIN and policy violation from the last 180 days—the time period that affects the account's AHR score. In theory, every seller should be able to appeal every policy violation and suspended ASIN. There is, however, a glaring exception: The seller cannot appeal if they do not have invoices. Needless to say, sellers must take steps to ensure they have invoices for every item listed on Amazon. But no invoices means no appeal.

Otherwise, it is worth the time and effort to appeal and thus maintain a high AHR Score. In addition to lowering the risk of account deactivation, successful ASIN appeals means:

- Sellers can continue to offer that inventory.
- Sellers will not have to remove, destroy or fire-sale the items on another platform

- Sellers will not lose money on their previously suspended ASINs, which can be margin-killers

If Amazon Suspends an Account, What Should the Seller Do First?

Take a deep breath.

The immediate reactions to an Amazon account suspension are anger, frustration, and downright fear. But like other serious challenges in life, success is more likely when the seller calmly outlines a strategy to solve the problem.

First, it's important to understand why Amazon closed the account. In most cases, the seller received an email as well as a notice in the Performance Notifications section of Seller Central. This notification includes a detailed explanation of why Amazon suspended the account. In addition, Amazon provides instructions on how to appeal, as well as the content required in the appeal.

In some instances, Amazon provides an appeal "button" for the seller to click in Seller Central. The next page shows dialog boxes with questions to answer. This is the format for the appeal Amazon has requested. When sellers read the Performance Notification and look at the appeal request from Amazon, a common response is, "but I didn't do it." Oftentimes, sellers assume that their suspension is based on false buyer complaints, evil competitor attacks, or a mistake. Occasionally, this can be true. But most often, Amazon has assembled plentiful data to justify the suspension and require a Plan of Action in response.

Enforcement against Amazon seller accounts is handled by Seller Performance. This department of investigators reviews complaints against sellers and account data—including metrics, feedback, and information that is not visible to the merchant in Seller Central. Yes, Amazon has a great deal more data than the seller about their very own account. Even if the suspension was over-enforcement or unfair, the seller must react in the way Amazon wants them to if they want their account back. Reinstatement is much more likely if the seller objectively analyzes the problem, takes responsibility, and provides an effective Plan of Action.

Account Reinstatement
Step #1: Understand the root cause

When Amazon asks for a Plan of Action, the first section is usually about the root cause of the problem. It's critical that the seller do a deep dive of their account and the situation at hand to ensure they truly understand why Amazon suspended the account.

Yes, Amazon suspended the account for late shipment rate or inauthentic items or forged documents. But why did these failures take place in the business? Did the shipping department fall behind because inventory wasn't available in a timely manner? Did buyers believe items were inauthentic because the product was matched to the wrong listing detail page? Did someone on the team submit a forged invoice without supervision and approval?

Amazon is a company of second chances for sellers. Even if the seller made egregious errors, there is a chance for reinstatement. But the seller must admit fault and explain in detail what went wrong.

Where should sellers look for information? They should check out store feedback, product reviews, Voice of the Customer, returns reports, and buyer-seller messaging for clues. In addition, any employees, virtual assistants (VAs), or service agencies that have been involved with the account should be questioned if their activities might cross over with the subject of the suspension. They should also check any external software tools that are connected to Seller Central to see if they have created risk.

Most importantly, the seller must take responsibility. There are always ways that an account can be improved, and those can be part of the Plan of Action.

Step #2: Make it right

Amazon wants suspended sellers to take steps to remediate the violation. In lay terms, this means to make it right. In the Plan of Action, Amazon specifically asks for steps the seller has taken to address the problem.

Orders that were not shipped should be shipped or refunded. Apologies should be made to upset customers. Bad supplier relationships should be cut off. In all cases, these steps must be concrete and provable.

Step #3: Prevent the mistakes from happening again

This is the meat and potatoes portion of the Plan of Action. Amazon wants concrete, measurable, and timebound steps to ensure the account doesn't stray into bad behavior again.

While this section of the appeal should be longest in most cases, it should still be to the point. Short sentences improve readability. Plain language is key. And the answers should be very specific.

After writing this portion of the appeal, the seller should ask a colleague, family member or friend to review the POA. If they cannot repeat back immediately what the plan outlines and how future suspensions will be avoided? It is time to start over.

What If Amazon Doesn't Respond or Rejects the Appeal?

Only a minority of seller appeals are accepted by Amazon the first time around. Often, Amazon asks for "more information." This could mean the appeal was not specific enough, or it could indicate that Amazon thinks the seller did not address the real problem in an effective way.

If Amazon rejects or ignores the appeal, the seller should go back to the beginning:

- Re-review all data and processes related to the topic of the suspension.
- Re-interview all personnel—both internal and external—who could have been related to the cause of the suspension.
- Review the appeal and look for disparities and how it may not have addressed Amazon's concerns.
- Be open to being wrong.

At this point, the seller can either submit another appeal to Seller Performance or attempt to escalate to an executive. Amazon embraces an escalation culture. Entire teams within

Amazon are dedicated to answering concerns from buyers and sellers about bad experiences, needs for help, and concerns about Amazon policies and procedures.

The escalation team or executive may or may not be interested in the Plan of Action. They may or may not be interested in the seller's personal story and circumstances. It is very important to match the email and Plan of Action correctly to the target of the communication.

Sellers must understand one critical point: spamming Amazon is unacceptable. If the same appeal is repetitively sent, the account is more likely to be blocked. If an off-point appeal is sent to multiple executives, the account is more likely to be blocked. Carbon copying and blind copying appeals to multiple contacts makes an account more likely to be blocked. Moderation is key.

When Should the Seller Hire a Professional Appeal Writer?

Companies like mine specialize in writing effective Amazon account appeals. We rely on decades of internal Amazon experience, as well as effective systems and in-depth knowledge, to help sellers understand why they were suspended. We assist them in developing a plan to address the problems, and then help them communicate with Amazon.

Many sellers opt to appeal for themselves the first time around for simpler suspensions, such as late shipment rate. But there are several circumstances where we recommend speaking with a pro and considering whether to outsource this task:

- If the seller's appeal was rejected, it may be time to hire a professional. Another viewpoint may be needed. Or the seller may not fully understand Amazon's rules and expectations. Multiple failed appeals can make it increasingly difficult to earn reinstatement.
- Certain suspension types should be an immediate red flag that prompts the seller to hire a professional. These include Section 3, Code of Conduct, fraud, forged documents, counterfeit, and platform manipulation. Amazon gives sellers fewer opportunities to appeal these suspensions and reviews these appeals to very strict standards. Sellers should not waste any of their chances. Hiring a professional is critical.

A final note on appeals. Frequently, when a seller's account is deactivated or blocked, they are tempted to simply open another seller account. In fact, Seller Support may have even handed out this terrible advice. Don't do it! This strategy will just make it more difficult to get the original account reinstated. In addition, if Amazon links the new account to the suspended account, they will both be suspended.

Who Gets Suspended from Selling on Amazon, Anyway?

Don't believe the Amazon boosters who say only "bad guys" have their accounts deactivated or their products taken down. As someone who works with suspended sellers every day, I take exception to this characterization of my clients and friends. It implies that anyone who loses their seller account deserves it.

Some sellers intentionally break the rules to get an edge or make a quick buck. Others unintentionally violated various Amazon mores because they didn't understand the rules, never bothered to learn them, or took bad advice. And some sellers are suspended because they are labeled with a "false positive," meaning that Amazon believes they broke the rules when they did not. Here are a few quick tales of woe that fortunately had happy endings. Learn from them!

Suspended—for no reason

I've always viewed my friend Connie as an ideal Amazon seller. She runs a small operation, doing 80 percent of the work in her Amazon business. Occasionally, she hires helpers during the busy season to help with shuffling inventory, organizing products, and packing orders.

Connie is Amazon's dream seller: She buys only legitimate products, with invoices or receipts for every single item; her recordkeeping is impeccable; and she carefully packs every item and includes personalized notes for buyers. If problems arise (and they rarely do), she takes care of the customer efficiently and with the goal of making them happy. She has a high repeat buyer rate. Connie also cares about the Amazon catalog. She spends dozens of hours a month correcting listings and ensuring that her products are accurately represented in the Amazon catalog. When I think about Connie as a seller, the word that comes to mind is "conscientious."

Connie's account was suspended. Why? Nobody knows. The suspension notice said that she had not provided a valid plan of action. But Amazon had never asked her for a plan of action. In addition, the suspension notice said there were specific ASINs involved. In the space where those ASINs should have been listed, there was blank space.

At Amazon, the department chiefly in charge of Risk Management is called Seller Performance. Connie reached out to Seller Performance and asked for more details. They responded by permanently blocking her account. Escalations to various executives were met with silence. Connie was burning through her savings and eyeing storage spaces packed with inventory she intended to sell in Q4.

I have two team members with thirty years of Amazon Seller Performance and Strategic Account Management experience between them. They reviewed her case and her account carefully, and they were baffled. They believed the suspension was a mistake, but that the account had been notated in such a way that nobody would give Connie a second review.

After weeks of suffering financially, mentally, and emotionally, Connie was finally reinstated. But it took multiple escalations to executives that, frankly, an average seller would never know to contact. Without that, who knows if or when she would have gotten her account back.

Frauded for weeks, then an apology

Jacob called us in a panic. He was completely locked out of the seller account for his small, family-owned business. He literally had no idea why. In Amazon parlance, he had been "frauded," meaning he could not log into Seller Central, and Amazon refused to respond to any emails or calls.

Jacob's business was gradually falling apart. A few years ago, his family decided to close their Manhattan store because of outrageous rents. They focused solely on Amazon, but they did not diversify further. Now, they were suffering as a result. Almost a month had passed since they were frauded, and they had to lay off employees. Their personal mortgage payments were about to be late, and their vendors were unpaid.

Jacob had tried several appeals and letters, but he had gotten nowhere. We took over and escalated to several executives. After a few weeks, Jacob received an apology from Amazon. It essentially said: "Oops. Sometimes we err on the side of caution. Sorry about that."

We have our suspicions about why the fraud designation happened. In all possible scenarios we dreamed up, it was a flat-out mistake by someone at Amazon. That mistake almost destroyed a multigenerational family business. We will never know the real reason for sure.

Wrongly accused of forged invoices

Ali sells replacement computer parts. Some customers complained about receiving these items in non-retail packaging, so Ali's account was suspended for suspected inauthentic items. He provided Amazon with detailed invoices from his supplier—a major distributor of PC parts and accessories.

In response, Amazon blocked Ali's account for forged invoices. Why? Your guess is as good as mine. Ali gave Amazon a supplemental letter from the corporate headquarters of his distributor, confirming his invoices are accurate. In addition, he sent Amazon stamped bank statements showing that he paid the invoices.

Ali is a good guy and an honest seller. Amazon continues to hold his funds and refuses to communicate with him about his account. How can this be, if only scammers are blocked?

Ali is not alone. Another client was accused of forged invoices because his supplier could not find a document when Amazon called him. The supplier confirmed three of four invoices, and he found the fourth only after the phone call ended. It took multiple escalations and a full month to get the "forged invoices" designation removed from the seller's account—even though none of this was his fault. A month is not "shortly thereafter." It's 8 percent of the year without sales.

Risk Matters

All businesses carry risk. And the best businesses address risk as part of their strategic planning process. You must understand the risks you face and act to mitigate those risks—not pretend like they do not exist. I realize that some consultants are only interested in Amazon boosterism, since they cannot sell their products and services to people who won't sell on Amazon out of fear. But isn't it more intellectually honest to provide a complete, accurate picture of what it is like to sell on Amazon?

If sellers don't comprehend the danger zones, they will fail in many ways. Why? They will believe that their good intentions are understood and accepted by Amazon, in place of following policy. Here are examples I see every week:

- New sellers start off by listing garage sale and thrift store products as "new." Amazon, however, expects receipts or invoices to be available for all new merchandise. This way, you can prove items are authentic and new. If Amazon asks for invoices and you don't have them, you're on a fast track to suspension.

- Sellers had an account closed in the past for breaking Amazon rules. It may have happened so long ago they cannot even remember the reason for the suspension. They open a new seller account for their legitimate business, such as a private-label brand. Amazon blocks the new account for being related to an old, suspended one.

- Sellers head to discount retail stores to find quick Amazon flips. They purchase large quantities of new inventory, and quickly sell through the items. When they receive a buyer complaint about item condition, Amazon asks them for invoices. The discount store receipts have a stock number and department code for each item, instead of a UPC and product name. The receipt is rejected, and Amazon suspends the seller account.

If new sellers understood how these techniques put them at risk, they may choose another business model. Successful Amazon sellers usually have at least a little capital available to get them started. All sellers need to also understand that Amazon can be a cruel mistress. We get the vast majority of our clients reinstated. But in all cases, sellers who are deactivated suffer from cash flow issues, lost revenue, and sleepless nights.

For the unfortunate few who are permanently locked out of Amazon, a scarlet A is not always deserved. Rather, kindness and understanding are demanded from those who comprehend how truly heartless the machine of Amazon has become.

5 Reasons Amazon 3P Sellers Need High Ethical Standards

Being honest has become one of the most critical values for Amazon sellers. Why? Because Amazon is increasingly cracking down on sellers who fib, manipulate, or otherwise break the rules. Here are some recent examples:

1. Amazon has begun wielding the big stick of "Code of Conduct" violations to immediately block seller accounts. These account closures are particularly challenging since they often do not fully inform the seller what rules were allegedly broken.

2. Suspensions for suspected forged or manipulated documents are increasingly difficult to overturn—even for honest sellers who sent in real documents but may have had some other problematic account issues in the past.

3. Amazon has silently partnered with textbook manufacturers and other brand owners to serve lawsuits against sellers who—knowingly or unknowingly—sold counterfeit or sketchy products.

4. Internally, Amazon has launched multiple investigations against staff members who were selling data and other favors to sellers. The sellers involved were summarily shut down.

5. Amazon is building on its history of going after sellers and service providers who use shady tactics and violate Terms of Service to "help" clients. A perfect example is the review-buying services that helped sellers purchase positive reviews for their products.

Amazon sellers are reasonably frustrated that Seller Support and Seller Performance don't live up to their promises. But in Amazon's eyes, that is all irrelevant. The seller still must provide authentic products at fair prices, stick to terms of service, and supply Amazon with whatever documents it requests.

Here are some rules to live by. If you currently cannot follow any of these rules, take the steps to put new processes in place—now.

- Have real, true, and unaltered invoices ready at a moment's notice. The failure to do this plagues a huge portion of our clients. Amazon expects that you be able to show the chain of custody for your products and prove their authenticity. If you can't, you will have problems. You need a true document management system to accomplish this, and all employees or agencies involved in answering Performance Notifications need access.

- Don't give in to the temptation to create fake invoices. Amazon has incredible technology at its fingertips. They will figure it out eventually. We've seen clients suspended even six months after submitting false documents.

- Set up a real quality control system. Your staff needs to know your products, inspect your products, and weed out the bad suppliers. Fakes are everywhere. You cannot sell them—even accidentally.

- Don't pay to play. We get the questions all the time: Can you help me pay someone to get my account back? Can you pay someone to get me ungated?

Can you help me buy a clean account? Our answer is always a resounding no. We cannot put our business at risk. But more importantly, we will not put you at risk of personal or business liability for corporate espionage activities.

- Know the terms of service and stick to them. Ignorance is not a defense. Amazon expects you to follow its rules about reviews, refunds, shipping . . . all of it.

Chapter 9 Summary

- Amazon expects third-party sellers to follow its rules—which are extensive and specific.
- If a seller breaks the rules, they may see their seller account suspended. ASINs are also taken down by Amazon for rules violations. This applies if the seller knowingly breaks the rules, unknowingly breaks the rules, or is the result of a false positive by Amazon.
- The Amazon appeals process can be frightening and difficult. Sellers may have to escalate their case to various internal teams and executives to get back on the Marketplace.
- It's important to maintain clean hands and high morals. Otherwise, you're setting yourself up for failure.

What about you?

1. Read the Amazon Business Solutions agreement. Take the time to fully understand Amazon's explicitly stated rules.

2. Visit the Help section of Seller Central. View the video tutorials. Read the basic rules. Search your product category or questions you've had in the past and read what comes up.

3. Do you have team members who work in Seller Central? Ensure they understand the rules for selling on Amazon. Require them to sign an agreement stating they will follow those rules, on pain of dismissal.

CHAPTER 10

The Marketing and Advertising Conundrum

If you list it, they will buy. Or will they?

You've arrived at Chapter 10, which means you've made great progress in your Amazon journey. Thus far, you've created a solid business plan, established operational strategies, and thought about how to source great products.

Next up, you need a killer marketing plan. On Amazon, even the best products do not sell themselves. Marketing and advertising are key to creating high-volume sellers on Amazon. But marketing and advertising look very different online than they do in traditional, brick-and-mortar retail businesses.

And at the behemoth of Amazon, sellers need a marketing strategy with basic, foundational steps before listing products and buying ads. These basics help ensure a healthy future for products you develop and are critical to your success. Let's walk through the unique and challenging Amazon marketing environment. First, we'll talk about the importance of trademarks and Brand Registry. Then, we will develop your product's marketing basics, including your unique sales proposition, branding and more. Then, we will translate these into effective listings on Amazon. And finally, we will talk about driving potential buyers to those listings.

Ultimately, you want to drive traffic to your listing detail pages, and then convert those viewers into buyers. Let's get started.

It All Starts with a Trademark

If you developed your own brand, you probably already filed for a trademark. Guess what? That won't protect you on Amazon—not really. You need to set up your brand the Amazon way, before you can create beautiful product listings or invest in ads.

Here's an example that explains why. After about thirty minutes of tense conversation about her Amazon account, a sob escaped Jana's lips. I could hear the beginnings of a total breakdown on the other end of the phone line. "But this is my product," she protested. "I designed and manufactured it with my own two hands. How can Amazon allow someone else to just rip it off this way?"

This upsetting scenario plays out daily for Amazon third-party sellers. They create and manufacture an exciting new item, and they launch it on the world's most powerful e-commerce platform. Once sales pick up, they become a target for counterfeiters. In Jana's case, an overseas competitor was selling fake versions of her product—on her listing detail page and her brand. But because Jana had not taken some basic steps at Amazon, she couldn't do much to stop it.

Fortunately, Amazon has devised a solution to help called Brand Registry. The key for sellers? Get a trademark on your brand as early in the process as possible.

There is an army of hijackers out there just waiting for successful new products to be launched on Amazon. I cannot even count the number of clients who have called me after a new seller suddenly popped up on their ASIN even though they had tight control of their distribution.

The majority of these hijackers are in China, although there are a fair number in other countries and the United States as well. Once a product starts to rank on Amazon and picks up substantial sales, the hijacker finds a manufacturer to create a knockoff version. They often use substandard materials and have lower product quality, so they can price their counterfeit product lower than the original.

This creates two significant problems. First, it steals sales away from those selling legitimate products. And secondly, it creates a passel of bad reviews, since the knockoffs don't match the product description and are of poor quality.

Amazon launched its Brand Registry to help sellers in these situations. With Brand Registry, a brand owner can:

- Maintain primary control over the Listing Detail Page, so other sellers cannot make inaccurate changes.
- Establish that their ASINs are authentic and legitimate.
- Kick hijackers who are selling counterfeit product off their ASINs.
- Create a beautiful storefront and Enhanced Brand Content on their product detail pages.

Essentially, Brand Registry helps brand owners establish and maintain some semblance of control over their brand on Amazon. It's not a perfect system, and the "bad guys" will always find work-arounds. But Brand Registry offers a reasonable solution for brand owners trying to stay a step ahead.

What is the key component of Brand Registry? It all starts with a trademark. Amazon requires brand owners to submit their trademark paperwork (via their attorney) and confirm that it is accurate. Only then can brand owners and sellers establish a Brand Registry account and control their ASINs.

This is why it's critical for private-label sellers to start the paperwork on a trademark as soon as it is established. It can take six months for the trademark process to be completed, and another two to three months for Brand Registry to be established after that.

When applying for Brand Registry, you officially own that brand if you provide proof of ownership. However, this does not mean that resellers and distributors will stop selling your product on Amazon. Brand Registry means product information across all listings will be consistent. So, while the seller owns the storefront, you control how the brand appears as a brand owner. It helps prevent competition because customers are more comfortable buying from the manufacturer or brand than third-party sellers. In addition, it allows brand owners to kick bad guys off their listings, if they are selling counterfeit products.

Amazon Seller Success Starts with a USP

Once you've got Brand Registry in process, it's time to develop beautiful listing detail pages that tell your product's story. To get started, you need a USP, or Unique Selling Proposition.

This helps an Amazon seller stand out from the crowd and attract customers. It's foundational to your marketing efforts.

The USP is a statement that communicates the unique value or benefit. It piques the interest and action of your target audiences. It's a brand message, a differentiator.

So, what is yours? Start by stepping back and digging into what is unique about your product. What message resonates with your target audience and what they want: their needs, preferences, and values?

The USP exercise is often treated like a weekend warrior who decides to walk around the block a couple of times vs. an athletic endeavor that requires time, discipline, training, and action. Developing the USP usually requires market research and analysis, such as surveys, focus groups, customer feedback, and competitive analysis. These undertakings help quantify what motivates your target audience, which then leads you to the unique value or benefit that really resonates.

What are the USP types?

It's free. A common USP (and often overused) is "free" and "fast." For Amazon sellers (FBM), that's usually related to shipping, which also helps compete with FBA's Prime delivery. Many customers are willing to pay a bit more for products that come with free or fast shipping. Frankly, is this really a USP in Amazon world where customers expect the product "right now," no matter what?

It's quality. Another common USP is high-quality products. Brands that emphasize the quality of their products, whether through materials, craftsmanship or performance, appeal to an audience willing to pay more for a product.

This is particularly important for products that are used frequently or have a significant impact on the user's life.

It's exclusive. Unique or exclusive products can also be a strong USP. Brands that offer products that are not available anywhere else, or that are only available in limited quantities, create a sense of exclusivity and urgency. These drive sales and customer loyalty. This is particularly effective for niche products (a specific demographic or subculture).

It's sustainable. Environmental or social responsibility is a growing USP for brands. Those that prioritize sustainability, ethical sourcing, or social responsibility appeal to customers concerned about these issues. The audience is willing to pay more for products aligned with their values. This often appeals to younger consumers.

It's personal. Brands that offer personalized, customized products provide a personal touch and sense of connection with the customer. This can be particularly important for brands offering highly personal or emotionally significant products, such as jewelry or gifts.

Getting started in developing a USP really means knowing, studying, and analyzing your customers. They are your target audience. What is the best way to do that? Talk to customers, ask questions, get honest feedback about pros, cons, strengths, and weaknesses. Do the research and delve into their needs, preferences, and values.

It's tempting to take shortcuts while developing a USP. It's easier to just be creative and come up with a powerful, pithy perspective. While it may be relevant, it is not your USP. It is not a creative exercise; it's a data-driven research project. It's also an ongoing effort, not a one-time event. Customers and market dynamics are always moving and evolving. So are your products and brands. Your USP may need to evolve as well. Regularly review and analyze customer feedback, market trends, and competitor strategies. Doing so helps establish a USP that could even expand into new segments and markets.

Once the USP is defined and delivered, it is a common thread woven into all your sales and marketing channels and touchpoints, from websites and email marketing campaigns to product collateral and tradeshow graphics. Your USP is strong, consistent, and ever-present.

The result? You have a valid, well-vetted USP that resonates with customers. It shares a consistent feature and benefit that builds customer familiarity, trust, loyalty, and reputation. Begin, then refine your USP. This ongoing commitment to know your customers—and knowing what motivates them to purchase your products—ensures your long-term success.

Build a Stronger Amazon Brand Identity

Building a brand identity on Amazon presents a unique set of challenges, even for the savviest private-label professional. But brand identity matters more than ever before. Once a seller has paid to acquire a customer via advertising, coupons, superior product development or promotions, the last thing they want is to lose a higher-margin repeat sale.

New private-label sellers on Amazon often are tempted to launch generic products. This is a bad idea. Amazon flat-out doesn't like generics. Instead, it's important to create a brand that will grace your products. That means after a trademark and a brand registry, you need:

1. **A unique logo.** This logo ensures that Amazon, its buyers, and competing sellers understand that the product is not generic. It also makes it more difficult for competitors to list counterfeit offers on your listing detail page. Ideally, the logo should appear on both the product itself and the product packaging.
2. **A brand guide.** The brand guide includes the brand's preferred fonts, colors, logo treatments, graphics styles and more. Setting this up from day one will ensure a unified look that buyers will begin to recognize and seek out.

Don't Phone It In on Product Packaging

Many Amazon sellers ship products that look completely generic when received by the buyer. This is a tremendous mistake. Why? While this may seem like just an extra expense for no added value, nothing could be further from the truth. Generic-looking items with no packaging or brown-box packaging are much less likely to inspire repeat buyers.

What's more, sellers shouldn't overlook future opportunities to take their Amazon-only brands to brick-and-mortar stores. That simply isn't possible unless packaging is both complete and attractive.

Design affordable, reasonable Amazon packaging that reinforces the brand's image, matches the product detail page, and looks unique enough to stand out in the minds of potential repeat and referral buyers.

Once these items are developed, it's time to invest in your Amazon storefront and listing detail pages. These are some of the most-neglected steps on Amazon, and this mistake plagues even established national brands missing out on sales.

The Keys to an Effective Listing Detail Page

The listing detail page is the "ad" for your Amazon product. At a minimum it features a headline, at least one photo, and a product description. The result of a bad listing is:

- Fewer conversions from people who click through to your listing
- Wasted ad spend from external traffic
- More sales for your competitors
- Low keyword rankings
- Negative customer reviews
- Poor category bestseller rating

Start by putting your listing detail page in the correct category. Amazon has dozens of subcategories that get very specific for various product types. By finding the exact subtype when you list your product, you will ensure that you maximize searches driven to your product.

Then it's time to create a listing detail page that isn't just informative, but also is highly optimized. Amazon listing optimization means ensuring you're covering all relevant keywords, your listing is set up to sell shoppers on your product, and your images clearly show your product and features of your product. Before spending anything on paid ads, ensure that the following are optimized: keywords, listing copy, and product images.

Dollar for dollar, money spent on listing optimization will create higher return on investment than almost any other activity on Amazon. Why? Listing optimization is the process of updating and changing the product detail page that will result in improving search visibility, click-through rate, and conversion rate. Together, this results in more sales. An optimized ASIN detail page can even work in concert with PPC campaigns to lower ACOS (average cost of sales).

This means spending the time and effort to ensure the page has:

- Relevant and targeted keywords in the title, bullets, and description, which create higher ranks in relevant searches. This results in improved traffic and clicks.
- High-quality images, which fill all seven available image slots for the page. These should include lifestyle images and infographics that educate customers to the point they are comfortable clicking "buy." The best lifestyle images usually include babies, dogs, or hot women. Shoehorn in two of the three for the best results.
- Bullets and a description that speak to the benefits and features of the product.
- A+ content (also known as Enhanced Brand Content) to create a more visually appealing and detailed product listing that also supports the overall brand.

Build a Beautiful Storefront That Shows Off Your Branding

Amazon allows sellers to create a heavily branded "storefront." This page features top products and allows ASINs to be sorted by category. It also enables brand owners to heavily showcase their brand imagery, logos, and other emblems that reinforce their unique branding for buyers.

Fully deploy the storefront feature, carefully following the brand book built out above. This shows buyers that products are not just being sold by a random reseller. They are being carefully curated and offered by a brand that cares about its image.

Get Moving with Beautiful Brand Videos

Amazon's search algorithm favors ASINs that feature high-quality videos in their listing detail pages.

Too often, sellers throw together ineffective videos that simply don't get the job done. These might show a product simply rotating on the screen or placed in a room. Do videos of that style create clicks and conversations? No.

For a great, brand-building video, ensure the brand book is included in the video-creation process. Include the brand's tagline, colors, logo, and messages. Make sure there is plenty of motion, and help buyers envision how they would use or enjoy the product.

Enjoy Your Amazon Honeymoon

Amazon loves new products—especially for thirty to sixty days. During that period of time, sellers enjoy a kind of honeymoon. These listings are favored in the search algorithm, and any sale dramatically impacts Best Seller Rank for the better. When launching a new product, be sure to do the following:

- Ensure your listing detail page is perfectly optimized. This includes keywords and photos, right from the start.
- Keep your price low. It's critical that you are priced favorably against similar options. You can always raise your price later—gradually.
- Offer coupons and sales. Take a few dollars off the price with these special features, which help shoppers notice that there is a short-term discount on the table.
- Advertise aggressively. During the honeymoon period, every sale counts. Take a loss if you have to, if it brings in new customers and boosts your BSR.

Figure Out What Works for Your Products

The sales and marketing mix is different for every category on Amazon. Test various features on the Marketplace to find the best solution for your products:

Amazon Vine. Product reviews drive more sales. But Amazon has super-strict rules that prevent you from asking family and friends for reviews or paying for reviews outside of Amazon. Don't have product reviews? Buy honest reviews with the Amazon Vine program. Unlike other purchased reviews, these don't violate Amazon's stringent Business Solutions Agreement. It costs about $200 per ASIN to enroll in the Amazon Vine product, and a maximum of thirty reviews is possible. The products are also supplied to the reviewer for free—meaning you are giving away products. It's still a pretty cost-effective way to jump-start honest reviews for your goods.

Coupons. These are one of my favorite strategies. Set up coupons with limited budgets. Coupons show up in search results, and prompt buyers to choose your product or purchase now. Sellers can limit the number of coupons, their value, set date ranges, and more. Generally, this is a very cost-effective strategy with strict controls.

Subscribe and Save. This fantastic feature allows buyers to set up a subscription, where they automatically purchase an item. Buyers can choose to refill their supplements every thirty days, or restock their paper towels every ninety days, for example. Building a base of Subscribe and Save customers by offering a solid discount creates far better return-on-investment than advertising ever could. This option is available for high-volume ASINs that are consistently in stock. Because you are getting repeat sales from individual buyers, the small discount offers a fantastic return on your investment.

Amazon Associates. This program allows content providers and influencers to drive traffic to listing detail pages. Seek out relevant publications, bloggers, and personalities willing to talk about your products. This can be extremely time-consuming and difficult, but it's an excellent strategy for a boot-strapping seller who doesn't have a lot of extra spending money.

Deals. Amazon offers Prime Day Deals, Deals of the Day, and 7-Day Deals. All of these are great options for sellers to move a large amount of product in a short amount of time. Sellers do, however, have to offer a substantial discount. During the deal period, the seller may only break even on sales made. But over time, there will be a benefit because of better sales ranking and additional reviews.

Pay-Per-Click (PPC) advertising. During your product launches, establish a generous budget, and continually test keywords to ensure the keywords are both on target and affordable. In the long run, continually monitor ad campaigns and make adjustments. Ensure your ACOS remains reasonable, or you will lose money.

Advertising comes last. It's a controversial statement, but one that I stand by steadfastly. Yes, pay-per-click Amazon ads can help drive your revenue and profitability on the Marketplace. But they can also destroy your margins—and drive your business into the red.

Competition on Amazon is fierce, especially when it comes to advertising. The cost of ads continues to rise over time. Instead of starting with advertising, what if you put it last on your to-do list? There are many more sensible ways to spend your marketing dollars first.

Chapter 10 Summary

- Many sellers jump straight to expensive pay-per-click advertising to move their products on Amazon. But for better return-on-investment, PPC ads likely should be last on the checklist of things to do.

- Amazon Brand Registry is the first step private-label sellers should take when launching new products or brands.
- The Honeymoon period offers an opportunity for sellers to quickly establish a better Best Seller Rating than expected, if their product launch goes well.
- Listing optimization, videos, Deals, Amazon Vine reviews, and other strategies all can drive traffic to listings over time.

What about you?

1. Do you have a Trademark for your products? If so, gather up the paperwork. If not, file as soon as possible!
2. Apply for Brand Registry.
3. Look at any existing listing detail pages you have for your products. How should they be optimized? What resources do you have to improve the photos, keywords, text, and Enhanced Brand Content?
4. Choose one new strategy to investigate for your products, such as a Deal or Coupon.

Part 4
Scale and Reach Your Goals

CHAPTER 11

The Magic of SOPs

You've taken major steps toward planning and launching your Amazon business, deciding everything from your Amazon avatar to your product sourcing and fulfillment. You've even put a risk management plan into place.

With all the focus on details, it's time to take another step back and ask a critical question. Do you want Amazon to be a business? Or a job?

Amazon as a job? It's a grind. There are so many details, processes, and everyday hassles. An Amazon seller who doesn't have structure and personnel in place can find themself chained to the computer, trapped in the warehouse, and continually reviewing the books.

There is a better way. With Standard Operating Procedures (SOPs) that you develop, your business can be more efficient and effective. They allow a business owner to push down tasks to virtual assistants (VAs) and other team members. With SOPs, the entire team is clear on the standard they should be working toward, the steps, etc.

There are many processes in an Amazon business that can be standardized via an SOP, for example:

- Fixing stranded inventory
- Answering customer service messages
- Creating FBA shipments
- Shipping out MFN orders
- Filing for reimbursements
- Sourcing products
- And more

Once you create an SOP, you can decide. Do you push this task down to someone on your existing team, hire a VA to handle it, or outsource it to an agency? The choice will be yours. As a business owner, my goal has always been to perform a task first myself, document and improve that task, build an SOP others can easily follow, push the work to a team member, and monitor its implementation. Then I start over with the next task.

How to Create an SOP

Creating an SOP involves several steps to ensure that processes are documented and standardized effectively. Here's a general outline of the steps involved in creating an SOP:

Identify the process. Determine which process or task needs to be documented. It could be a routine task, a complex process, or a critical operation within your business.

Define the objective. Clearly state the objective or purpose of the SOP. What outcome or result should the process achieve? Having a clear objective helps focus the documentation and ensure it aligns with the intended goals.

Gather information. Collect all the necessary information related to the process. This may involve observing the process in action, interviewing subject matter experts, reviewing existing documentation, and capturing relevant data.

Break down the process. Analyze and break down the process into smaller steps or subtasks. Identify the sequence of actions, decisions, and interactions involved. Ensure that each step is clear and concise.

Document the steps. Write detailed instructions for each step of the process. Use clear and simple language, avoiding jargon or ambiguous terminology. Include any necessary diagrams, visuals, or screenshots to enhance understanding.

Include key roles and responsibilities. Identify the roles and responsibilities of the individuals involved in the process. Clearly define who is responsible for each step, who needs to be informed, and who has decision-making authority.

Document tools and resources. Specify the tools, equipment, software, or resources required to perform the process effectively. Include any guidelines, templates, or reference materials that employees may need.

Test and validate. Test the documented SOP by following the instructions and performing the process. Validate its accuracy, clarity, and effectiveness. Seek feedback from stakeholders or subject matter experts to ensure its completeness and usability.

Review and revise. Regularly review and update the SOP to reflect any changes in the process, technology, or best practices. Ensure that it remains up to date and relevant. Involve key stakeholders in the review process to gather their input and insights.

Communicate and train. Share the finalized SOP with your team. Conduct training sessions or workshops to ensure that everyone understands the process and knows how to follow the documented instructions.

Implement and monitor. Roll out the SOP across the organization and monitor its adoption and effectiveness. Track metrics or key performance indicators to evaluate the impact of the SOP on process efficiency, quality, or other desired outcomes.

Continuous improvement. Encourage feedback and suggestions from employees who work with the SOP. Continuously evaluate and improve the SOP based on lessons learned, new insights, or changing business requirements.

Remember that the level of detail and complexity of the SOP may vary depending on the process and its importance to your business. It's important to involve the relevant team members, communicate effectively, and ensure ongoing maintenance and updates to keep the SOP working and useful over time.

My Favorite Amazon SOPs

After more than a decade selling on and consulting about Amazon, I've developed a set of SOPs that I believe are some of the most effective for sellers. They save time, ensure rules are followed, and generally make life easier. Following are these favorites, which I hope are helpful for your business.

Create an invoice storage/filing system for your Amazon ASINs

It's critical that sellers have always-on access to their invoices. Why?

- Buyers sometimes complain to Amazon that a product is inauthentic/counterfeit, or that it is sold in poor, not-new condition. Amazon suspends the ASIN and asks the seller for invoices proving that the product is authentic and new.
- Amazon suspends a seller account and asks for invoices during the appeals process.
- Amazon "gates" a seller, preventing them from selling in a category or brand. To appeal for ungating, the seller must present invoices.
- Amazon fails to receive inbound FBA shipments, or Amazon FCs lose or damage inventory. When the seller files for reimbursement, sometimes it's necessary to provide invoices to recoup funds.

Unfortunately, many sellers are completely disorganized and cannot provide invoices when requested. You must have all invoices easily accessible for Amazon. But you also need them for tax purposes, and to close your books! The same standards and filing system SOP should be applied to all product documentation, including safety, testing, etc.

Here's a quick-and-dirty SOP for always having invoices on hand:

- Gather up all invoices and receipts for this calendar year. This should include both electronic and paper documents.
- Scan any invoices that are not already electronic.
- If you have a lot of receipts, consider using a receipt and invoice scanning service like Shoeboxed.
- Determine whether your current bookkeeping software has functionality that allows you to store invoices within it.
- If you do not wish to use software for this, use nested folders on your PC or an online storage system such as Dropbox, Google Drive, or Microsoft OneDrive. If you have VAs or agencies that need access to your invoices, use some kind of shared drive.
- When items are purchased, immediately add them to your storage system.
- Use descriptive titles for invoices, with ASINs if possible, so correct invoices can be found quickly.
- When providing invoices to Amazon, it is acceptable to highlight the individual product and add the ASIN, if it's not clear from the context.
- Be sure that more than one person has access to your invoices. For example, we've had sellers go on vacation, and while they were gone, Amazon asked them for

invoices to be provided within seven days. Someone needs access at all times.

Amazon has high standards for accepting invoices:

- The document must be clear and easy to read.
- The name of the buyer on the invoice must match the name on your account.
- Addresses also should match.
- Amazon oftentimes researches the supplier, checking for a website, valid address, and more.
- The quantity of products on the invoices must be equal to the quantity sold on Amazon in the last 180 days.

Forged documents are a fast-track to a permanent block of your Amazon seller account.

No matter who tells you to "spiff up" those invoices, just say no. As happens all too often at Riverbend, I was assigned a ticket for a new client who was suspended for forging documents. During our call to discuss his account, he assured me that he had done nothing wrong.

"Did you ever edit an invoice?" I asked. "Well, yes, but it was OK to do," he answered.

I didn't follow his reasoning and pushed for more details. "I have an account manager at Amazon," he explained. "They told me to edit the documents to fix the dates and quantities, so it should have been fine."

This is pretty common in forged documents cases. Our clients feel justified in manipulating invoices because they believe they are somehow presenting the "spirit" of what actually occurred in their business. But Amazon doesn't want an approximation. They want actual, true invoices.

Other circumstances where we've seen forged documents include:

- The seller has multiple accounts and ordered merchandise under one company name, while selling it under another company name.
- The seller bought items from a "friend," rather than from a distributor, wholesaler, or manufacturer.
- The seller failed to obtain proper invoices—ever—from their supplier.
- The seller sold more items than they have invoices to cover. This could be because they first conducted test buys or obtained samples.
- The seller is worried about their invoices being from more than 365 days ago.
- The seller is buying shady goods.
- The seller created a false invoice to get ungated because they didn't want to buy the minimum for new inventory that they may not be able to sell.

In any of these circumstances, do not give in to temptation and submit a faked invoice. Just don't do it. You are much more likely to be successful with Amazon by explaining the circumstances of your less-than-ideal invoices. On the other hand, if you forge invoices, it's extremely difficult to convince Amazon to give you another chance. They will simply not trust you again. And for good reason.

Build the SOP. It will be worth it.

Clean out your Amazon catalog listings

Sometimes Amazon takes down a product for being a "restricted product." When this happens, it's critical that sellers not continue selling other ASINs that have the same restricted product problem as the ASIN Amazon suspended.

For example, if a supplement is removed from the Amazon catalog because it has an ingredient now prohibited by the FDA, it's important that the seller delete any other products with that same ingredient—even if Amazon hasn't suspended those ASINs. The same goes for other categories, such as items Amazon has declared are drug paraphernalia, items with unacceptable or pornographic images, etc.

Consider it a warning that Amazon removed the first ASIN and do the responsible thing to clean out related and similar items before Amazon does. If you fail to remove items with the same violation, you are endangering your account. Amazon can suspend a seller account for restricted products if they detect repeat violations or a failure to remove similar products to those suspended by the safety team and Seller Performance.

The SOP for this situation is simple:

- If you receive an ASIN suspension for restricted products, determine if you believe it is justified.
- If you believe it is not justified, appeal the situation with Amazon. If you fail in your appeal, move to the next step. If you succeed in your appeal, you're good to go!
- If your appeal failed or the product should, in fact, be restricted, get clear about why.

- Have a team member search your catalog of products on Amazon. Find any that share the same characteristic that got the restricted product suspended.
- Place removal orders for all inventory at the FBA warehouse.
- Delete the product listings. Don't just close them. Delete them.

Sanitize your inventory regularly

Many sellers never delete a product from their inventory. They just leave it there. Forever. This is a dangerous move. Why? Because if you have an item in your inventory—even with zero units available—Amazon believes you have the intention to sell it again in the future.

If an ASIN is recalled, if it's declared a restricted product, or if it otherwise violates a rule sometime in the distant future? You could be held responsible.

This SOP is simple but critical. Set an appointment on your calendar for once a week, once a month or once a quarter, depending on how many items are in your catalog. Delete anything you don't intend to sell again in the future. It's that easy.

Keep inventory selling

Stranded inventory can be the bane of any seller's existence. Unfortunately, getting inventory from "stranded" back to "active" can be difficult, time-consuming, and frustrating.

But every day that inventory sits in stranded, a seller has their cash tied up—rather than making sales and using the proceeds to buy more inventory or rake in profits.

Whether you use an in-house employee, a VA, or an Amazon service agency, it's critical that sellers have a strategy in place to get inventory active ASAP. In some instances, a few clicks in Seller Central will solve the problem for a well-trained employee. In others, a case with Seller Support must be opened, monitored, and followed up multiple times. And sometimes, appeals are needed to address product quality issues or policy violations. No matter who is tackling these issues, they cannot be allowed to linger. It's far too expensive—even if this expense seems hidden.

Always be improving your worst ASIN

Some Amazons sellers have two or three products. Other sell thousands, tens of thousands, or even hundreds of thousands of SKUs. But all these sellers have something in common: they have one worst ASIN. Take away that worst ASIN, and they will still have one worst ASIN.

Bad ASINs can cause a multitude of problems, from poor reviews to high return rates to safety concerns and more. Add these problems together and suddenly, the ASIN loses money. It doesn't have to be that way.

I recommend that sellers continually work to improve their worst-performing ASIN:

- Uncover which ASIN is losing the most money, generating the most returns, or generally causing expensive headaches.
- Rehab that ASIN.
- If the ASIN cannot be affordably rehabbed, scrap it; don't sell dogs.
- Repeat with the new worst-performing ASIN.

Start by determining which is your worst ASIN. Collect data for the trailing thirty days of sales:

- Run your FBA and MFN returns reports in Seller Central. Sort the spreadsheets by return reason. Remove orders with return reasons for which you're not at fault, such as "ordered by mistake" or "undeliverable." Calculate the adjusted return rate for each ASIN.
- Review feedback in Voice of the Customer on Seller Central.
- Review seller feedback, product reviews, and the Account Health dashboard.
- Review buyer-seller messaging.

In all these cases, you are looking for quantitative and qualitative data indicating which ASIN should be of greatest concern to your business. A fast-selling ASIN with moderately bad performance will trump a slow-mover with horrible performance. Focus on the product doing the most damage to your bottom line.

Based on the data gathered above, choose a strategy to improve your worst ASIN. Improvements can then come in the form of:

- Updating the product detail page to clarify information that is confusing to buyers
- Requiring stepped-up inspections at the manufacturing facility
- Improving product packaging so the item arrives to the buyer in perfect condition

- Redesigning the product for its next manufacturing run
- Improving FBA prep
- Asking FBA for better fulfillment center packaging
- Improving MFN shipping methods or prep
- Stop selling the product

Never, ever give up on improving your worst ASIN. Improved them all? Start over again!

These incremental, continual improvements are hard work, but they are what separates high-margin, successful brands from the flashes-in-the-pan. And while driving more revenue and profitability, these improvements also will keep sellers out of the Amazon suspension doghouse.

All these processes can be distilled into an SOP that can be performed by a VA or other team member over time. Based on the size of your catalog, you may choose to improve your worst ASIN every day, every week, or every month.

How to Get Results When You File a Case with Amazon

Sellers get frustrated when they open cases with Seller Support. Why?

- Canned answers that don't solve the problem
- Cases being closed without a resolution
- Freestyle responses that make no sense
- Reopening cases again and again and again—still no resolution

If you want an answer, follow these steps:

1. Start with a clear ask. State what you need help with in a single sentence.
2. Explain what you already did to try and solve the problem. Make these bullet points.
3. State why it's important the problem be solved. If possible, link this to a benefit to Amazon or an Amazon buyer, instead of you and your account.
4. Restate your request for specific assistance.

If you get another nonsense response, reopen the case. Firmly and kindly say that your case was not answered satisfactorily, and you don't believe anybody actually read it and took the time to try and solve it.

Above all:

- Be kind.
- Be measured.
- No temper or foul language.
- Be understanding. It's hard to provide customer service for sellers and answer technical issues.

MFN Orders Piling Up? Go on Vacay!

It's important to understand the metrics Amazon expects from MFN sellers—and how to keep out of trouble. Amazon requires a late shipment rate of less than 4 percent and an order cancellation rate of less than 2.5 percent.

Follow these tips to ensure you don't run afoul of Amazon's rules:

- Check your stats every day. Watch them like a hawk.
- Get out every order by the promised ship date. Don't rely on third-party software. Actually look in Seller Central to see which items are not shipped out, and get them out ASAP.
- Ensure that you get an origin scan by your carrier. Amazon doesn't consider the order shipped unless it is scanned.

If you even start to feel behind, go on vacation. You can do this in settings in your account. Temporarily pause accepting new MFN orders until you are caught up.

What happens when you run out of inventory or simply mess up and need to cancel an order? You want to ensure that you don't get negative feedback. Try these strategies:

Don't leave them hanging. Buyers don't like it when you make them wait past the estimated ship date. If you figure out you won't be able to ship, cancel sooner rather than later. Be timely and apologetic regarding cancellations. Don't wait. Explain that you are cancelling the order immediately so that the buyer has time to place a new order with someone else.

Explain the problem. When cancelling an order, buyers understand the truth and a valid reason why the order must be cancelled. For example, suppose a tornado shut down your operations. Send a message stating that a weather event happened today in your location. Since the safety of your employees is paramount, you are not requiring staff to come in today so that they can prioritize their families.

Don't confirm then cancel. Buyers don't like it when sellers confirm orders, only to cancel them and issue a refund. This is technically mail fraud. In addition, buyers become very angry when an order is cancelled, yet they can see that it is still available for sale on Amazon.

What should you do long-term? Ensure you have staff redundancy to fill orders even if your regular MFN staff are not available. And be sure that someone can put your store on vacation via mobile if your infrastructure is not functional.

All these MFN strategies can be turned into simple, understandable SOPs for your order fulfillment team. And keep you out of trouble with Amazon and with buyers!

Chapter 11 Summary

- Sellers who want to build a valuable business—instead of a J-O-B—must create SOPs and push down processes as much as possible.
- Follow a careful process when building and implementing SOPs. You are stuck with the results long-term.
- SOPs for storing invoices, prepping and grading inventory, going on vacation, and more are critical to the success of an Amazon business.

What about you?

1. Make a list of any existing SOPs you have in your business. How can they be improved? Are they being followed?

2. Find your worst ASIN! Create an SOP that others in
    your business can follow to always be improving your
    worst ASIN.
3. Survey your operations and make a list of every possi-
    ble SOP you can think of that might help over time,
    or when personnel turn over. Prioritize these and make
    a plan to create one SOP per week.

CHAPTER 12

Outsource It

You're on a roll! You've gotten this far in planning your Amazon journey, and now it's time to expand your vision. Up until now, you've been learning about your tasks as an Amazon business owner. You've created a vision, chosen an avatar, and developed a business plan. You've contemplated products, marketing, and operations.

But now new challenges arise. Payroll keeps rising. Competition gets stiffer. The need for specialization in tasks like brand management, account health, and advertising grows every day. Which of these functions should sellers handle in-house? For very large businesses, the answer might be to keep everything under the corporate umbrella. But for small and expanding sellers, the correct choice may be to outsource almost everything.

Here's where the rubber meets the road. Outsourcing enables Amazon sellers to reach their visions and goals faster and easier—without working a hundred hours a week. Plus, outsourcing keeps costs under control.

As your business develops, the need to outsource some of your tasks becomes increasingly evident. The dramatic benefits of outsourcing can be destroyed, however, if you don't know how to hire competent service providers. And even more importantly, you must know when to bestow access to the keys to your Amazon kingdom. Making wrong decisions can put your business in jeopardy.

Common Outsourced Relationships for Amazon Sellers

Amazon sellers who scale successfully generally do so by choosing a combination of in-house resources, best-in-class service providers, and virtual assistants. The trick is understanding what should be outsourced, and which type of resource should handle each task.

For most of these work items, the potential outsources are an Amazon agency or a virtual assistant (VA). By outsourcing, sellers can avoid human resources expenses that include recruiting, onboarding, benefits, and more. Plus, they can ensure continuity by relying on a full-featured firm with an entire team of employees to service their account. Some agencies offer the best of both worlds. Rote tasks such as customer service messages are handled by a lower-cost, offshore team of virtual assistants, and yet still supervised by a US-based team of managers to ensure consistency, continuity, and quality.

Essentially, if you can write a quality Standard Operating Procedure (see chapter 11) for a task, it's ripe for outsourcing to a VA. If a process is technically difficult, changes frequently, or relies on complex if-then processes? You're probably better served by reaching out to an experienced Amazon agency. Commonly outsourced tasks for Amazon sellers include:

Amazon FBA reimbursement services. These providers comb through a seller's FBA inventory to find all instances where Amazon lost, damaged or otherwise misplaced inventory. They file and follow up on cases in Seller Central. Reimbursements providers can find thousands of dollars even for small sellers.

Amazon buyer-seller messaging. VAs and agencies can take on the task of replying to Amazon customer queries. Some providers even help sellers create and update template messages over time. These teams answer within Amazon's preferred twenty-four-hour window, provide refunds and return labels, and more. Customer service messaging is most valuable for MFN sellers, who tend to receive more emails from buyers.

Customer feedback and review management. When customers leave negative store feedback, it is often eligible for removal. A good VA can get inappropriate feedback deleted by Amazon and provide positive replies when needed. In addition, both positive and negative product reviews can receive replies. This time-consuming task is best left to an outsource that understands the tricky rules for reviews.

Account Health. Amazon sometimes suspends accounts and ASINs. Appealing these situations can be technically difficult, require domain expertise, and often need escalation to various Amazon teams to reach a positive resolution. Agencies can take on these challenges as they arise, or they can monitor a seller's account and address ASINs on a day-to-day basis.

Listing optimization. Sellers can outsource listing optimization tasks to experts who specialize in keyword research, copywriting, and content optimization to improve product rankings and conversion rates. Photography and graphic design can be part of the optimization equation as well.

Amazon advertising management. Running effective pay-per-click (PPC) advertising campaigns on Amazon requires continuous monitoring, optimization, and keyword research. Sellers can outsource Amazon PPC management to specialists who have expertise in managing ad campaigns, bidding strategies, and keyword optimization.

Fulfillment services. Sellers may choose to outsource fulfillment to third-party logistics providers (3PLs). These providers can handle inventory storage, order fulfillment, shipping, and returns management—either for Amazon FBA or FBM. High-quality 3PLs can also streamline operations, reduce stockouts, and ensure timely fulfillment.

Social media and marketing. Sellers can outsource social media management, content creation, and digital marketing activities to agencies or freelancers specializing in social media marketing. These experts can create and manage engaging social media campaigns to drive brand awareness and customer engagement.

Accounting and bookkeeping. Managing financial records, bookkeeping, and tax compliance can be complex for Amazon sellers. Hiring an accountant or outsourcing bookkeeping services can help ensure accurate financial reporting, tax filings, and financial analysis.

What to Look Out for When Hiring an Amazon Service Provider

When your business reaches full-scale mode, you may be bombarded by different Amazon service providers vying for you to outsource some of your mounting tasks to their solutions. Each service provider may require different access to your Amazon Seller Central account. The more you know about the service providers you choose, the better you'll be able to monitor the health and safety of your account. The wrong provider can cause an Amazon account suspension. For example:

- A private-label brand hired a full-service agency to manage their account. The agency submitted forged invoices to Amazon, resulting in Amazon account suspension.
- An FBA business hired an untrained independent virtual assistant to file Amazon FBA reimbursements on the business's behalf. The VA filed duplicate reimbursement requests forcing an account suspension.
- A business used an untrained VA to answer customer service messages. The VA became frustrated and wrote abusive messages to customers, causing buyer-seller messaging to be turned off by Amazon.

To hire the best service provider, it's essential first and foremost to understand the business model of that service provider. Review these five criteria before hiring:

1. Experience level. How long have they been in business, and how many clients have they helped? How many

years of Amazon selling experience do the owners have? Can they provide case studies and professional references to match? A professional case study isn't clouded with fancy terms that don't mean anything. Professional case studies accurately depict the situation, the challenge, and the results delivered. Hard numbers and customer quotes are a bonus. Avoid providers who only offer fluffy content, as this can be a red flag.

2. Supervision model. Everything in your account boils down to trust, communication, and experience. Who is the last point of contact before large account-level decisions are made? What are the safeguards of the supervising team? Who do the supervisors report to? Does the service provider have USA-based team members with experience in Amazon? By using onshore supervisors, you can reduce the number of communications issues, while improving the level of oversight and the likelihood that Amazon's Business Solutions Agreement (BSA) is being followed.

3. Standard Operating Procedures (SOPs) and communication. The only way to know if an Amazon service provider operates with stringent SOPs is to ask. Inquire about SOPs and policies and get a sense of the growth trajectory within the business. An Amazon service provider with a clear understanding of their own growth path is more likely to operate a successful business model. A reputable provider should have a standardized method of doing business. This is not only so you receive the best, most consistent service, but also so that if things go wrong, there are procedures in place to follow.

4. Non-disclosure agreements (NDAs). Are NDAs standard for the service provider? Confidentiality is everything to your Amazon business. NDAs are a must, not a maybe.

5. Transparency and compliance with the Amazon BSA. What are the service provider's safeguards within their team, and how do they enforce compliance? Can you see different stages of work being completed at any time during your business together? While you have a responsibility to uphold Amazon's terms of service independently, so does your service provider. Your service provider should be able to discuss BSA compliance with you before onboarding. If a service provider breaks Amazon's rules, the enforcement doesn't happen against them. It happens against you and your account.

You may not be comfortable asking service providers these questions, but think about it this way: professional businesses will accept these questions as a normal part of doing business with you, especially because they understand the associated risks operating within your account.

Don't Set-It-and-Forget-It

Yes, outsourcing exists to take responsibilities off you and your Amazon business. But that doesn't mean you can walk away from the tasks and not ensure they are happening properly. Clear communication will be your best friend in terms of working with various e-commerce consulting services. Ask for a consistent communication path based on your needs.

Good communication examples are weekly Zoom meetings, quarterly reports that detail advancements and challenges in your business, and instant communication channels such as Slack. You'll want to dedicate time and focus to attending these meetings and reviewing each report. As much as a service provider should be responsible to provide transparent information, it's crucial that you are an active participant in your business. Keep up to date on the inner workings of your business with any service provider to keep your account safeguarded at all times.

Sadly, we see too many Amazon seller accounts suspended for inadequate safeguards in working with service providers. Often the service provider's workforce is working with little to no SOPs resulting in unnecessary account suspensions. Or there is inadequate communication and supervision from the account owner. It's important to ask questions with any service provider that you onboard from virtual assistants to consultants to large-scale reimbursement companies and other service providers. If a service provider shows hesitation in answering your questions, this may be the right time to pause and re-think your direction.

Amazon-Provided Services or an Independent Outsource? That Is the Question

Amazon's premium "support" services for sellers and vendors are an expensive, unmitigated failure. Fortunately, there are better options for your business.

Amazon 3P sellers and vendors resort to paying for the company's premium services in hopes of solving their Amazon problems. These overpriced options rarely give the desired results. Instead, choose consulting services with accountability, customer service, and results.

The e-commerce dominator recently has stepped up its hard-selling techniques for both of its high-priced service packages:

- Strategic Account Services—Core (SAS-Core) was designed for Amazon's third-party sellers. The service costs $1,600 per month plus 0.3% of a seller's total sales in the prior month. Fees each month are capped at $5,000.
- Amazon Vendor Services is offered to top-tier members of the Amazon Vendor program. Pricing starts at $250,000 per year, but it can run to $1 million or more.

What do sellers and vendors receive for their hefty payments? According to the hundreds of clients we've discussed this with, not very much. Spoiler alert: Many 3P sellers and vendors can pay much lower fees to outside agencies and get much better results. Most importantly, these agencies can be held accountable by your team. (Amazon and accountability don't belong in the same sentence.)

Wouldn't it be great to have your very own Amazon account manager? That's the big draw for SAS-Core. Amazon claims that these magical unicorns will work directly with 3P sellers in the SAS-Core program—and they "only" manage twelve to fifteen accounts at a time! Work closely with your account manager to "prioritize your next steps that can have an impact on your sales." You get a monthly call to review your business plan and "come up with tailored action items each month." These amazing experts will provide advice in "key areas like fulfillment and inventory, account health, selection and conversion growth, merchandising and advertising, and global expansion." Plus, they can help with listing creation and detail page recommendations. How about one-on-one coaching and mentoring too!

Wow. Those are some super-skilled account managers who know everything possible about running a successful Amazon account. Ahem. In case you missed the sarcasm, there's a reason that the open market is filled with specialists in particular Amazon subject matter areas. Entire agencies are dedicated to Account Health challenges, PPC advertising, fulfillment, and inventory management, etc. The idea that a single person at Amazon has the in-depth expertise to advise across all these areas in an in-depth, value-added manner is nothing short of ludicrous.

Most 3P sellers we've spoken to who signed up for SAS-Core specifically wished to have Amazon insider help if and when they had a problem with a suspended account or ASIN. Since the SAS-Core team is supposed to help solve critical issues, their reasoning made perfect sense.

Unfortunately, many users of this premium service are sorely disappointed by a combination of Amazon's internal policies, lack of training and know-how on the part of SAS-Core reps, a lack of reasonable and fast internal escalation paths inside of Amazon, and just plain old bad customer service similar to what you might see with Seller Support.

In many cases, the seller can pay my firm far less in fees than they pay for Amazon SAS-Core. We solve their problems when these "Amazon insiders" could not or would not.

On the flip side of the Amazon coin, Amazon Vendor Services (AVS) is an invitation-only program for top-tier vendors. Only high-volume performers could afford the program's massive price tag. AVS promises to improve listing content, improve listing searchability, increase customer reach, and drive up conversion rates.

For example, a vendor came to us with a serious problem. They own several brands, all of which are part of Amazon Brand Registry. Despite this, unwanted and inaccurate changes were continually being made to their listings by third parties. The results were disastrous. ASINs had been pulled down as Restricted Products, for example, because inaccurate ingredient information was added to the detail page. The vendor reached out to Vendor Relations to ask for help. Ultimately, a Vendor Manager said this: "These Brand Registry problems are frustrating. If you would like us to fix them, you can join our AVS program for $1 million per year."

That's right. The Vendor team essentially said they would not provide basic, reasonable, and critical customer service to ensure this brand's listings were not being wrongly edited by others. But for a cool million, they might find the time to fix it all.

There are lots of words that might describe this "sales pitch." None of them are positive. Regardless, others who are part of AVS have expressed many pain points with the program. It features poor customer service, badly trained reps, extreme delays in addressing critical issues, and a refusal to address financial issues such as overcharges and underpayments by Amazon.

Forget spending $1 million with Amazon. A vendor can hire an outsource firm to address many operational issues, plus hire an agency to manage their catalog, inventory and more. And they will have cash left over.

Pay for Real Results—and Accountability

Agencies and consulting firms offer several critical advantages over these costly Amazon programs:

Accountability. It is literally impossible to hold account reps, account managers and other individuals at Amazon accountable. There are many reasons for this, but the end result is all that matters. Even if you are an eight- or nine-figure seller, you do not have the ability to set standards or performance expectations. You are the little guy, and you are at their mercy.

Results. If you submit a request for help, nobody at Amazon is focused on truly ensuring you get results. In contrast, a consulting firm is deeply invested in helping its clients get the end result they need.

Customer service. The Service Level Agreements (SLAs) at SAS-Core and AVS have little meaning. At consulting firms, adhering to SLAs is a key performance indicator. Another huge differentiator? You can get agencies on the phone! Amazon just doesn't want to talk to you. Period.

Ungating, Platform Manipulation, and Black Hats —Oh My!

Amazon sellers beware. People will lie to get into your pockets—and destroy your Amazon account in the process. Every week, we meet new clients whose Amazon seller accounts were suspended for some form of platform manipulation, review manipulation, Code of Conduct violations, or forged/manipulated documents. In many cases, these suspensions happened because of service providers who claim their offerings comply with Amazon's Business Solutions agreement. Clearly, they do not.

It is a sad reality of the Amazon Seller space:

- There are high-quality service providers and software tools.
- There are functional service providers and software tools.
- There are charlatans who take money under false pretenses and put sellers' accounts at risk.

In the charlatan category, three examples of risky propositions come immediately to mind:

- Ungating services
- Tools designed to drive reviews or boost Best Seller Rank (BSR)
- Black Hats who pay bribes to Amazon employees or attack competitors unlawfully

Consider ungating services. Amazon sometimes "gates" a seller out of a category or brand, meaning they are unable to sell those items. Amazon then asks the seller to apply for approval to sell the items in question. The application typically includes a request for invoices that meet Amazon's high standards. Ungating services claim to help sellers get approved for high-demand categories or brands—without actually purchasing relevant ASINs and providing legitimate invoices.

For example, a client came to Riverbend Consulting with a daunting suspension. Amazon deactivated their seller account for forged or manipulated documents after they hired an ungating service. The service boasts on its website that all its documents are authentic and can be verified by Amazon. Sadly, that is a lie. Ungating services often falsify invoices and submit them on behalf of the seller. To understand why, it helps to know how ungating services work:

- The seller gives the ungating service a third-party login to their account.
- The ungating service creates an application for the gated category, brand, or ASIN.
- The ungating service magically obtains the exact invoices needed by the seller for approval by Amazon.
- The ungating service submits these documents to Amazon, which may be fooled into approving the application or may detect that the documents are fake.

Why do I assume that the documents are fake? Simple. Amazon wants invoices that demonstrate a true, completed transaction between the seller and their supplier. When sellers use an ungating service, no such transaction has taken place. The ungating service is either creating or obtaining false documentation. Perhaps they are altering real invoices. Or perhaps they have cultivated employees at supplier companies. They may pay bribes for false invoices, as well as paying someone to answer the phone, pretending they are the supplier and confirming to Amazon that the invoices are real.

Whatever method they use, this behavior is both unethical and against Amazon's BSA. It can result in immediate account suspension or a permanent block. Worst of all, this particular ungating service used a generic Gmail address for the third-party login on each and every seller account. This put every past client of theirs at risk of suspension. Amazon Seller performance could easily perform a search for accounts with that login email address and reasonably assume that the ungating service submitted false documentation for them as well.

As this particular service admitted to our client on a chat, hundreds of their clients' accounts went down. That didn't prompt them to take down their website or stop selling their scam service to new customers.

Other risky outsourced services fall into the category of platform manipulation. Several software vendors have stepped into this unsavory space. They "help" sellers improve their Best Seller Rank (BSR) or gain reviews by:

- Featuring products on "deal" websites, which link to Amazon. Buyers can get products at steep discounts. This boosts sales volume inorganically.
- Using chat bots to offer free products or refunds after a review is posted.
- Providing refunds to buyers who purchase products, so they essentially become free after-the-fact.

Amazon considers all these strategies to be inducements to write positive reviews and/or an inorganic way of boosting BSR. Services like rebates and deal sites are used either to boost reviews or boost BSR artificially. Amazon will never assume that a seller was wanting to give away some free product out of the goodness of their heart. They know these strategies are intended to increase positive reviews or BSR, and they act accordingly. Amazon is also acting in accordance with the rules of the US Fair Trade Commission. Amazon must legally act when they find abuse of their platform, regardless of how or where the seller manipulated reviews or BSR.

The hucksters that sell these services will claim that nobody gets suspended for using rebates, launch services and discount sites. That is simply not true. My consulting firm has worked on hundreds of platform manipulation suspensions because sellers were using these and similar tools. Some scammers even claim that Amazon has "approved" their services, which is something that Amazon would simply never, ever do from a risk management perspective.

Finally, there are the Black Hats of the Amazon ecosystem. Some bribe Amazon employees so that their "client" has a positive result. Bribes are paid for account reinstatement, ASIN reinstatement, account notations, ungating, and more. Other Black Hats work with overseas click farms and other bad guys to hurt the competition. This includes modifying competitors' ASIN detail pages with pornographic images, offensive descriptions, or prohibited words. False reviews, fake upvotes, false orders that are returned, extortion . . . the possibilities are endless.

In both cases, using a Black Hat service can result in countless bad outcomes for sellers:

- Loss of selling privileges
- Lawsuits from Amazon or other sellers
- Criminal charges
- Civil charges filed by government agencies

How can sellers avoid being caught up in this terrible net?

- Be aware of arrests and indictments in the industry. You wouldn't hire an accountant who was charged with tax fraud. It's too risky to hire an Amazon consultant who was charged with bribery and wire fraud. Being aligned with them puts your account at risk.
- Never work with a consultant who offers to obtain Amazon's internal account notations. This is illegal.
- Never work with a consultant who explicitly or implicitly speaks of bribing Amazon employees.
- Avoid any schemes to interfere with your competitors. Using overseas operations in China, Russia, and Eastern Europe doesn't make these actions any less illegal. And yes, ultimately, they can still be traced.

Save your money. Save your account. Avoid these risky services.

Chapter 12 Summary

- The key to scaling on Amazon is to outsource activities that are repetitive, time-consuming and prevent sellers from growing rapidly. These should be managed via a Standard Operating Procedure, or SOP.
- Additional activities that are ripe for outsourcing include complex, difficult and hard-to-manage activities, especially those that lie outside of the account owner's personal expertise.
- Before hiring an outsource provider, ask questions. Ensure that the company has guardrails in place to

comply with Amazon's Terms of Service. Check to see that all activities follow predetermined SOPs.

- Avoid Black Hats and other bad actors, especially those who offer to obtain account notations. It's just not worth it.

What about you?

1. Analyze your current Amazon operation. Which low-level activities are taking too much of your time and headspace? Are you willing to find an outsource for these tasks, whether it's a VA or an agency?

2. Which complex and difficult Amazon account activities make you most nervous? What is hardest for you to complete and manage? Are you willing to outsource these tasks?

3. Make a list of these activities that could be outsourced. Start searching for service providers. See if you can gradually outsource each area on a schedule, perhaps one per quarter. Monitor each activity as it is taken over by a service provider, to be sure your standards are being met.

CHAPTER 13

Hit Your End Goal

If you've read this entire book, you know one thing for sure: Learning about Amazon is like drinking from a firehose. The topics expounded upon between these covers encompass only a portion of what it means to be an Amazon seller. Ongoing learning and continuous improvement are the only paths to success in the Marketplace.

For new sellers, you may be overwhelmed by the breadth and depth of information thrown at you. We made checklists. We answered questions. We made you reconsider all your goals and life choices. It was a journey! For experienced sellers, you probably took away ideas for new processes and SOPs. You learned about Amazon enforcement and some other freaky details of the Marketplace.

In either case, what should you do now? We've all read business and self-help books. And in the end, how much do we really implement? In my own experiences, failure to implement the ideas from a book I found helpful wasn't the fault of the author. Rather, I received the advice when I had no structure to put it into practice.

Like you, I'm an entrepreneur. My life is full—very full. I'm a co-founder and co-owner of two growing, successful consulting firms. I own an Amazon selling business. My husband

and our two sons are intelligent, spirited, and adventurous men with unique ambitions of their own. They each have ventures that I try to assist them with, just as they have all three worked in my enterprises. On top of that, I volunteer with my favorite charitable organizations. And I'm launching my own not-for-profit that will work to help kids with cancer.

I'm sure your life is similar. Amazon business owners are "my people": hard-working, over-committed, excited about taking on new challenges, and ready to succeed. I'd like to offer you some of my favorite non-Amazon strategies that have helped me to reach key goals. These are all geared toward entrepreneurs like you and me, in hopes that you can use them to implement the ideas in this book!

Begin with the End in Mind

Okay, I admit it. "Begin with the end in mind" is a trite, overused, and even annoying phrase. But it holds kernels of truth. By setting goals, you are much more likely to get to a happy place.

The realist in me gets frustrated by goal setting. Too often, I have to alter my goals, plans, strategies, and tactics. But editing these is so much better than operating without them!

If I can convince you to revisit one portion of this book, it is Chapter 5. Hustlers, goers, and doers tend to skip right to the action items. We don't spend enough time dreaming, imagining, and wishing for the future we really want to have. Can you escape your normal environment for a long weekend alone, or with your significant other? If not, can you set aside a date night to dream? Build that vision board. Consider those HARD goals—the ones that get you excited about what you can accomplish for yourself, your family, and your community.

Also, consider the real end-goals for your Amazon business specifically. Do you want it to sell for millions of dollars? Do you want to run it for the foreseeable future, creating a good income to fund your dreams? Pick a path and move that way.

Make a Strategic List

Books give too much information, especially the first time through. That's why I included handy summaries at the end of each chapter, as well as a list of questions for you to answer. Set a timer for fifteen minutes. Now flip through the "What about you?" sections at the end of each chapter. Write down three to five tasks you could take on this week that would move your Amazon business forward.

Why do this? Because easy wins matter! Moving forward, even in the small things, will inspire you to do more. After those wins, do it again. Repeat. Find a chapter that speaks to you. Reread it and make an implementation list. You can do it!

Get Through Each Day

No matter how many goals, checklists, or plans we have, days sometimes just slip by. It takes hard work to prevent this from happening. For me, the key has been establishing consistent routines. Key elements include:

- Exercise before anything else—outside if possible. Eat something healthy. It matters.

- Complete some combination of reading, prayer, and meditation.
- As part of meditation, focus on that vision board! Think about goals. Don't let a single day pass without pondering your short-term, mid-range, and long-term goals. It makes a tremendous difference.
- Maintain zero-inbox for both email and snail mail. I used to think this was impossible and insane. Now, I understand how it dramatically improves my productivity.
- Finish operational busywork and critical meetings before noon every day.
- Leave afternoons as open as possible for deep work. This might include developing SOPs, training team members, sourcing products, writing, and dreaming up the next big idea.
- Reach out to at least one friend or business acquaintance a day for a casual, positive conversation.
- Stay off screens that aren't adding value to your life in the moment.

Routines must be individualized. I share mine only to give an example—not to tell you how to live the day-to-day of your life. If I were implementing ideas in this book, I would most likely focus on those in the afternoons, during my deep work time.

Be Ruled by Your Calendar

To reach goals on time, you must be a slave to your calendar. Throughout this book, I mentioned certain processes and

SOPs that should be performed once a week, once a month, or once a year. I talked about goals that should be set and followed up on after a particular period of time has passed.

The only way to meet these goals is to hold yourself accountable with the calendar. An accountability partner wouldn't hurt, either!

The Ultimate Expansion: Take Your Winning ASINs to Brick-and-Mortar Retail

For many brand owners, one of their stretch goals is expansion into brick-and-mortar stores. They want to get the most out of their marketing investment and experience the thrill of seeing their products on the shelves of a physical retail store.

There are significant financial and risk management benefits to this strategy. It creates a separate stream of income from the Amazon business. It also reduces overall risk because goods can sell in stores even if they are suspended and removed from Amazon. Plus, online sales benefit from in-store brand recognition, and vice-versa. Finally, a seller is paid back for their manufacturing run of products one order at a time on Amazon. When making a sale to a retailer, they are paid for the entire delivery of goods at once—typically in thirty to sixty days. This can enhance the overall cash flow needed to grow a brand and manufacture more units in a timely manner. It can also create additional methods to obtain financing via factoring and other secured loans.

Here is what retailers want to see:

- Data showing that you have had significant sales success online.

- Beautiful branding, as well as a brand portfolio of multiple products that might work in their stores.
- Effective packaging for a retail shelf, which may not currently exist for products sold only online.
- Knowledge of strategies such as endcaps and point-of-purchase displays—and how your product can effectively fit into and work in a retail store footprint.

There are a great many challenges to getting into retail stores. Understanding these will help you plan for the future as your Amazon business grows and expands:

- Relationships with buyers in retail chains
- Relationships with the right buyers in the right departments
- Knowing whether to launch your existing high-end brand into a retail store or create a diffusion brand, which has a lower price point and adjusted branding.
- Understanding how to set up your vendor number.
- Obtaining capital to manufacture enough product for retail orders, or financing to underwrite the orders.

The best strategy? Find a business that specializes in taking online products to brick-and-mortar retailers. You get only one chance to launch correctly at a retail chain, and going it alone can be risky.

Find Your People

Selling on Amazon can feel isolating.

If you're an accountant, a bartender, a teacher, or an engineer, it's easy to find your people. There are other accountants, bartenders, teachers, and engineers in your community. They are living on your street, attending your church, members of your club, or coworkers past and present.

Amazon is a different animal. I've known sellers who did not meet another Amazon seller in real life for years—until they chose to attend an Amazon conference or join a local meetup group. When other folks ask what they do for a living, it's not unusual for the response to be, "I've never known anyone who sells on Amazon."

Man was not meant to be alone. That goes for professionals as well. Entrepreneurs and business unit managers can learn from one another. We need each other's ideas, wisdom, and experience. There are hundreds of "tips and tricks" that can improve an Amazon business. The Amazon community is largely filled with open, kind people who will share their knowledge. You just have to be in a place to receive it.

Yes, there are many online groups to join. But nothing takes the place of actually interacting with others. Some online groups have webinars and virtual meetings. There are in-person industry conferences, some of which focus on smaller sellers and others where content is geared toward the big boys. Local meetups are a great place to start for those focused on RA, OA, and wholesale sourcing. For private-label sellers, mastermind groups are an excellent choice. No matter which you choose, consider these hints:

- Attend as many online events as possible to learn about the industry.

- Immerse yourself in the online groups, where people ask and answer questions.
- Attend at least one live event each year.
- Make a friend or two who are in similar categories or of similar size and will be facing the same issues.
- Take advantage of non-selling discussions about personal challenges, finances, and lifestyle.

Get Help When You Need It

As I mentioned earlier, selling on Amazon can be an isolating experience. Don't go it alone.

Experts in this industry love to share their knowledge. Reach out to them—including me!—on LinkedIn or Facebook. Introduce yourself. Ask questions. Visit their websites—including mine!—and sign up for their newsletters and other content. Read their blogs. Watch their YouTube videos. The resources are endless.

Amazon—and folks like me—are here to help you succeed and create a life of your dreams. Never, ever give up.

About the Author

Lesley Hensell is cofounder of Riverbend Consulting, whose eighty-five-plus employees solve critical problems for sellers on Amazon and other e-commerce platforms. She is also a partner in Project Retail, which helps Amazon sellers place their winning products in brick-and-mortar stores. With help from her husband and sons, she has been an Amazon seller for more than a decade.

A lifelong Longhorns fan, Lesley earned a bachelor's degree in journalism and an MBA from the University of Texas at Austin. In her free time, Lesley supports Texas-based nonprofits that serve the pediatric cancer community. She volunteers for A Wish with Wings, a wish-granting organization for little Texans with life-threatening conditions. In addition, Lesley serves on the Board of Directors for Hallie's Heroes, which funds bone marrow matches, medical research, and expenses for kids with cancer and other critical illnesses.

Acknowledgments

I am deeply grateful for the love, support, and assistance of my household of men—Henry, Austin, and Jackson. Without their consistent help and patience, there would be no Riverbend, no selling on Amazon, and no book. We are not just a great family—we are a great team.

My team of Riverbenders are my source of Amazon knowledge, memes, and daily motivation. Thank you to each and every one of you.

Much appreciation to my superstar editor Michael Campbell, who "found" me, made my manuscript stronger, and made this book happen.